BRITISH
INTERROGATION
TECHNIQUES
IN THE SECOND WORLD WAR

BRITISH
INTERROGATION
TECHNIQUES
IN THE SECOND WORLD WAR

SOPHIE JACKSON

The
History
Press

First published 2012

The History Press
The Mill, Brimscombe Port
Stroud, Gloucestershire, GL5 2QG
www.thehistorypress.co.uk

British Library Cataloguing in Publication Data.
A catalogue record for this book is available from the British Library.

ISBN 978 0 7524 6271 4

Typesetting and origination by The History Press
Manufacturing Managed by Jellyfish Print Solutions Ltd.
Printed in Malta.

CONTENTS

INTRODUCTION

A war can be won or lost on information. Believing the wrong rumour or disbelieving the right one can have devastating effects on a country's war effort.

Yet the intelligence network of Britain was a late bloomer. First used to great effect in the First World War, between the wars, what would become MI5 was dismantled, disregarded and disposed of. When the Second World War broke out there was a scramble not only to re-enlist useful intelligence men from the last war, but to find new candidates.

The result was that the first organised British intelligence agency began to take shape. The British were novices at the spy game, though fortunately so were the Germans. Blunders and mishaps marred the early days, but with the urgency of war people quickly honed their skills and soon Britain's secret service was not only impressing Churchill, but also our enemies in Germany.

The highest compliment our system received at the time came when German interrogators chose to adopt some of our techniques when interviewing enemy prisoners and spies.

What shone out in the eyes of the Germans were our methods of interrogation. We seemed to have ways of wheedling the smallest detail from men and then turning it against them. Franz von Werra, the famous Nazi escapee, would be stunned to discover how much his British captors knew about him; down to his pet lion cub's name and an injury to his finger.

But none of this happened over night. Techniques developed and were often adapted from disastrous mistakes. Departments were created and staffed by a close-knit team of men and women, but often they fell prone to rivalries with other teams and constant backstabbing dangerously undermined successes. Spies were turned or executed. Prisoners were wrung for useful military secrets. Alien civilians were examined for potential treachery, and all this largely on an ad hoc basis.

Without the men and women who spent those war years examining reams of information and sorting the useful from the irrelevant, talking to endless captives, listening for hours to hidden microphones to catch a snippet of useful knowledge, Britain could have easily lost the war. Yet while spies and espionage have often been glamorised and portrayed in film and television, the quiet work of the interrogators has largely been forgotten outside of academic tomes.

Although it may not at first seem as thrilling as spying or sabotage missions, a spy, at the end of the day, is only a man relaying information – a man who must rely for his own safety on those interrogators working in cramped rooms night and day gathering reliable information.

The story of interrogation has been sidelined, yet the interrogators were the true heroes of the intelligence game, without whom no spy could have succeeded, no military deception would have been believed and no army could have marched secure in the knowledge of where the enemy was. Indeed, it could be argued that interrogation was the key to winning the war.

I

BRITAIN VS. GERMANY

Imagine a small cell, painted in uniform grey, the only furniture a heavy table and two chairs opposite each other. A bare bulb swings from the ceiling and minimal light comes in from a heavily barred window. A man (or woman) is escorted into the room by unsympathetic guards who deposit their charge in the nearest chair. In the far chair an unassuming man sits, perhaps bespectacled, but always with a calculated smile and a file of papers before him.

He sets forth a series of questions to his prisoner, which are stonily ignored so, with a grin, he begins describing various tortures and, when his victim continues to withhold their information, he sets about acting upon his threats. A huge number of Hollywood movies, television dramas and books can now fill in the gaps when it comes to the imaginative tortures inflicted on our 'hero', whether they are a spy, criminal or a Second World War soldier.

This is the typical image the word interrogation brings to mind; a picture reinforced by recent revelations of Guantanamo Bay and popular media. It has become stereotypical that should any hero, real or fictional, be captured, they should expect physical torment, and that image is strongest from the Second World War, with Germans usually portraying the evil interrogators.

Ironically, however, torture was not as prolific in the war, either on British or enemy soldiers, as is commonly portrayed. There is no denying it occurred, but the evidence for it being a universal practice in the interrogation services is simply not there. In fact the best and most successful interrogators, British or German, refrained from torture, deeming it 'unproductive'. Lieutenant Colonel R.W.G. Stephens, the fearsome commandant of British Camp 020, where numerous spies and suspect civilians were interrogated, was clear on his views of torture: 'Violence is taboo, for not only does it produce an answer to please, but it lowers the standard of information. There is no room for a percentage assessment of reliability.'[1]

Torture was therefore viewed as the tool of amateurs or the inefficient. What reliability could be placed in the words of a man who has been made to confess under physical duress? It is an age-old question that has been asked time and time again, whether during the seventeenth century witch trials or the early days of interrogation in the First World War.

These views were not the enlightened opinions of peaceful men who abhorred violence, however, they were ideas bred from practicality. Stephens knew what others would come to realise: torture provoked easy answers, but not necessarily true ones. It was considered a great failing of the German intelligence services that they relied so heavily on blackmail and violent threats to gain information and recruit spies. Those same spies were so easily turned by their British interrogators that it was almost laughable; once out of the clutches of their Nazi masters they willingly divulged their missions.

Unfortunately. a minority did not share Stephens' views. The London Cage, headed by Lieutenant Colonel Scotland, became infamous for its supposed use of physical torture, and even Stephens detested his counterpart Scotland, who was banished from Camp 020 after hitting a recalcitrant suspect over the head.

The same applied in Germany; there was no universal code for extracting information in either countries, and both British and German interrogators were free from limitations other than those of their conscience or pragmatism. The cases of Bad Nenndorf, mentioned in a later chapter, show that the British could equal the Gestapo and Nazi concentration camps for violence and lack of humanity.

While for the British these detestable practices were the rarity, it was often the reverse in Germany. Why these two countries diverged in their information gathering is as much a case of culture as a case of the fledgling system of intelligence gathering. The early history of spying is vital to the understanding of the interrogators' role and attitude.

How to Build an Intelligence Service

It is strange to realise that intelligence gathering as an organised body is really the creation of the twentieth century. The game of spying is as old as civilisation, but the organised compiling of the information these men and women found, and the interrogation of enemy agents, is relatively new. Prior to Queen Elizabeth I diplomats or courtiers were expected to pick up useful information from reliable sources and pay for it out of their own purse. It was not exactly a system and certainly not efficient or reliable. That all changed with the appointment of Sir Francis Walsingham in 1573, the iconic spymaster who excelled at the game of information gathering.

Walsingham's greatest triumph was successfully ending the war against Spain and the defeat of their armada, in part achieved by his intelligence network. Unfortunately his success was spying's downfall, and the lack of a significant enemy threat made intelligence gathering rather redundant. Throughout the history of the intelligence game it has always been the case that in peace it is neglected, only for that neglect to be regretted when another war threatens seemingly out of nowhere. Various leaders failed to realise this lesson. Cromwell employed spies to gather news on Catholic Spain before attacking them, and then proudly declared his superior intelligence system had enabled the victory. Yet once again, as soon as conflict ended the system was disbanded.

For the next two centuries British agents were a loose band of individuals employed by whoever footed the bill. The government's creation of the Secret Service Fund was commonly tapped into by MPs wishing to fund their election campaign or bribe other MPs (Lord Bute stole £80,000 for this purpose). No wonder the British people saw the secret service as a money-making scheme for corrupt politicians. This view was not helped when Irish Republicans began a bombing campaign in England in an attempt to gain Irish independence, and the intelligence service was unable to cope with the new threat. Even so, it took the Boer War to convince the War Office that they needed a properly developed and maintained intelligence service.

When Britain found itself in an arms race with Germany, for the first time intelligence gathering was viewed as a true priority. In 1909 the Security Service Bureau was established with Captain Vernon Kell of the

South Staffordshire Regiment and Captain Mansfield Cumming of the Royal Navy heading it. Despite being formally recognised, Kell still found his service woefully undermanned. He only had fourteen staff to deal with finding and arresting German spies and counteracting espionage prior to the First World War. The government was regularly, and rightly, accused by intelligence men of failing to recognise the importance of the system.

Meanwhile, Germany was also developing a network of intelligence agents and spies, whom it regularly attempted to get into Britain. Twenty such spies were rounded up by Kell before the outbreak of the First World War, but he was still aware that a large spy ring was in operation and that useful information on the Royal Navy was being relayed to the kaiser. The spy ring could have had serious repercussions for Britain had one of Kell's officers not overheard a chance conversation on a train in 1911. The conversation concerned a strange letter received from Germany by the proprietor of the Peacock Hotel in Leith, wanting details of Britain's war preparations. The Germans presumably considered the proprietor a possible agent, though his confusion suggests he was not the man they wanted.

In any case, he was interviewed and agreed to allow future communications to be intercepted by Kell's team. Through this not only were Kell's team able to develop a scientific means for reading the secret ink the Germans used (which would be invaluable during the war), but on 4 August 1914, as war against Germany was declared, they were able to launch an operation to arrest twenty-two enemy agents. All but one were caught and interned. It was a deadly blow against German intelligence and Kell was rightly proud of his success.

Yet capturing a spy was only half the story. Without a dedicated band of interrogators who could work tirelessly to extract information, uncovering an espionage suspect would have been difficult. Confirming his (or her) guilt and wringing military secrets from them would have been impossible (or, at least, a hit-and-miss affair).

The Security Service Bureau became MI5 in 1916, but a name change did not give Kell any new powers. The service, as it is today, was purely advisory. Arrests and interrogation had to be left to the police, perhaps with MI5 agents looking on but without the ability to interfere. It was frustrating for those working at the forefront of intelligence, but their hands were tied.

The main interrogator of the many suspects MI5 brought to the police was Sir Basil Thomson, Assistant Commissioner of the Metropolitan Police. Typical of his age, Sir Basil had little time for 'foreigners', was deeply patriotic and damning of the Germans: '... it is characteristic of the German mentality to underrate the intelligence of other nations and really to believe that anything German must be *uber alles*. It was largely owing to this self-satisfied obtuseness that they lost the war.'[2]

He possibly had a point and certainly his views would be carried over into the Second World War, when Lieutenant Colonel Stephens made similar comments about the German Abwehr and the state of their spy network. Yet it could also be argued that these same interrogators, who condemned their enemies for being arrogant and self-confident, suffered from exactly the same syndrome. In any case, Sir Basil was laying down the foundations and guidelines that two decades later his successors would follow.

Interrogators maintained a strong sense of honour and patriotism and respected this in enemy agents. More favour and sympathy was shown to a spy who served Germany because he believed in the cause than in a spy who was merely working for money. Spies that cracked too easily or willingly offered to switch sides were viewed with such distaste that often interrogators seemed all too eager to have them sent off to the firing squad or gallows.

The patriotic German spy Hans Karl Lody struck a particular chord with Sir Basil and drove him to declare that it was a crying shame that a distinction could not be made between spies driven by patriotism and those by money, and that the former could avoid execution. Lody was described in glowing terms as he faced his firing squad, and 'died as one would wish all Englishmen to die – quietly and undramatically ...'[3]

In fact Sir Basil broke a cardinal rule that Stephens and other Second World War interrogators would insist upon – he became friendly with an enemy agent. When the interrogators of twenty years later questioned POWs and suspected spies it was always with professional and conscientious detachment, but then they had learned from the errors their predecessors had made. The First World War interrogators were, in many respects, having to make it up as they went along. They were in new territory and while the police may have been used to questioning criminals, it was a far cry from questioning men trained to betray an entire country. Even at this early stage those working in intelligence were frustrated with the minimal training the police interrogators were given. They did not have the knowledge to deal with espionage suspects and many of those sitting on the outskirts watching longed to get into action themselves.

One such man was Lieutenant Colonel Alexander Scotland. He would later become notorious as the commandant of the London Cage, but he learned his art on the battlefields of France in the latter years of the First World War.

Scotland began his career spying on the German military in South Africa and he claimed proudly to have 'infiltrated' the German army. In fact he was a supplies agent for them, given an honorary military rank to enable him to move about the army lines more easily when delivering goods. But it was typical of Scotland to exaggerate his involvement and to come across as single-handedly winning the intelligence war.

With the air of someone who had grown up on boyish adventure stories, but the appearance of someone more suited to sitting behind a desk (Scotland readily admitted that his outward appearance was 'least impressive'),[4] he offered himself to the War Office to serve as an intelligence man and was promptly turned down. It took some persistent wrangling and heavy name dropping before he was finally accepted and sent out to France. In actuality, Scotland did have some highly useful assets – he was fluent in German and from his time in the German army in South Africa was familiar with their various protocols and procedures, something that regularly baffled the other British intelligence officers.

His first mission was to go to a prisoner transit camp at Le Havre to try and answer the rumours that the Germans were rehabilitating sick soldiers and getting them back to the front far faster than the British could. Intelligence needed to know if this was true and whether it meant the Germans were already feeling 'the pinch' in their manpower.

Scotland approached the problem laterally; instead of confronting each man individually with questions he assembled them on parade and, speaking in German, summoned the senior NCOs. He then issued them with paper and pencil and instructed them to work through the other men and ask each one if he had been in hospital, the nature of his injuries and how long he had been out of action. Two hours later he had a stack of grubby, but legible, papers with the information he wanted. By midnight they were in the hands of a dispatch rider and heading for GHQ. Scotland remarked: 'It seemed to me a reasonable reflection that the war could not last long if only the direction of affairs were left in my hands!'[5]

Modesty indeed! However Scotland's efforts did earn him the accolade of German experts at GHQ, and he now spent a great deal of time interrogating prisoners. He was a natural intelligence officer with a knack for holding on to the smallest detail and thinking on his feet. He could bend his mind around corners if he needed to and knew when flattery or tact would work better than force. In the later controversies that emerged about him, his earlier skills were obscured; possibly with age he found it harder to keep pace with prisoners and to out-think them, thus resorting to violence and abuse. But that is for a later chapter.

Scotland started to build the basis of a true interrogation system out of the prison camps in France. Unlike Sir Basil, who allowed familiarity and fondness for a prisoner to get the better of him, Scotland always maintained distance and kept in mind he was dealing with the enemy – a tactic that Second World War interrogators would readily adopt as part of their professional guise.

In 1916 he was sent to a camp called The Cage, which was used for prisoners from the Somme. There was a field hospital right next door for both British and German casualties. It was here that Scotland employed his methods in what he called 'the first war crime'. A German plane flew over The Cage one night and dropped several light bombs on the field hospital, wounding numerous people and, ironically, killing one of their own comrades who was having emergency surgery on the operating table. The surgical section took a direct hit and the German patient stood no chance.

A short time later a pilot was captured and brought into The Cage, and Scotland instantly suspected this was the culprit (largely based on the man's 'sullen, shifty expression').[6] Getting the man to admit to the crime was another matter. Normal questioning failed and the Prince of Wales started breathing down Scotland's neck for results. He decided to escort the enemy pilot to the ruined hospital and show him the body of the dead German patient. Making it clear this was the direct result of the bombing the pilot broke down; this was enough proof of his guilt for Scotland, though the pilot later escaped trial by committing suicide.

On another occasion, when he questioned a German oberleutnant, he was more tactful in his approach. The oberleutnant, who arrived at The

Cage with a letter of recommendation from the Australian troops who had captured him, had apparently led his machine-gun unit in such fearsome resistance against the Allied soldiers that he held them up for four days.

Scotland realised this man would be likely to resist normal interrogation and, due to his dogged determination that had so impressed the Australians, it seemed disrespectful to single him out for interview and chance the scorn of his fellow prisoners. So Scotland walked to the prison tent with the letter, asked for the oberleutnant to step forward and announced to the prisoners that he had a letter from the Australians praising the man's bravery. He explained he wanted to know more about the incident, and the oberleutnant left the tent with his fellow prisoners smiling at him approvingly.

Praising the man in front of his comrades had the desired effect, and when Scotland began talking with him he was open enough to talk of his upbringing in South Africa. Another piece of luck now presented itself to Scotland and he pounced on it; he happened to know of the oberleutnant's father. Aided by this coincidence the conversation quickly developed and soon they were talking about German morale and the state of the country; the prisoner never suspected that four men were stationed around the outside of the tent with notebooks, taking down every detail.

Thus Scotland had already mastered two of the most common tactics of the interrogation service – confrontation and conversation.

However, the end of the war brought a familiar conclusion to the intelligence (and therefore the interrogation) system. Most of the interrogators, who had perfected their skills in France on enemy prisoners, were stood down, including Scotland, who went with characteristic bad grace. Meanwhile, Vernon Kell at MI5 started clandestine infiltrations of communist cells with a staff that had been reduced to barely a dozen. He firmly believed that Bolshevism was the biggest threat to peace and that Hitler was not about to launch another intelligence offensive against Britain. Germany could, effectively, be ignored.

Kell's disastrously misdirected attentions had a number of causes; in part he had been separate from the First World War working to uncover spies in Britain not talking to the various German officers who were being interned in France. Kell thus had a one-sided view: spies were either paid mercenaries or extremists, and could be written off as the minority. Interrogators in Europe, however, could talk to thousands of men and learn how prevalent the idea of rebuilding Germany and thus starting the war all over again was, especially among the officer ranks.

Other factors influencing Kell were that Russia was a turbulent power, their agents more organised and discreet, and more feared than German spies who were often viewed as bumbling and inadequate. How accurate this view was is debatable, but throughout both wars and peacetime the Russian espionage threat was often deemed greater and more dangerous, simply because their agents proved harder to corner.

Kell was also swayed by his warm feelings for Hitler – the same warm feelings that much of the aristocracy were developing – and the growing fascist threat stemming from Mussolini in Italy, which started to take priority in the 1930s with the rise of British fascist movements and the 'fifth column' scare.

For others the misinformed efforts of Kell and the government were frustrating. Scotland fumed after a luncheon meeting in 1939 with various London executives who spent the meal voicing idiotic, pro-Nazi views. He had had the misfortune of meeting Hitler and had to wonder how close he had been to being another of the dictator's casualties. He also had in-depth knowledge of the rising German power and the danger it posed.

Scotland was so infuriated he wrote a detailed report on the Nazi threat and offered to lecture on intelligence and interrogation for the War Office. He was quietly declined with a postcard acknowledging the receipt of the paper.

When war did break out there was yet another scramble to rebuild the intelligence services of the First World War. In 1940, now aged 60, Scotland was called up to head an interrogations department and set to work picking POW campsites in France where interviews could be carried out. He was disgusted by the woefully under-prepared British army in this regard. With the exception of one or two men who had some experience of intelligence work from the First World War, his new employees were pathetically under-trained and had no concept of how to interview Germans who came through their camps.

MI5 was equally struggling. While the staff had been increased to thirty, it was nowhere near enough manpower to deal with the extra work of the war. They were simply drowning in paperwork – reports, vetting requests and enquiries overwhelmed them, and during the second quarter of 1940 they were receiving 8,200 vetting requests each week alone.[7] Civilian internment also took its toll on resources, with 64,000 people of various nationalities being detained (all having to undergo security interviews), and then there was the fifth columnist fears and the surveillance of suspected Nazi sympathisers, such as Sir Oswald Mosley.

Kell's health rapidly declined with this increased workload; the easy pre-war days discussing potential communist threats and ignoring Hitler were gone. Perhaps his previous brush-off of the Nazi threat was the final nail in his coffin, for when Churchill came to power in 1940 the prime minister fired Kell with little formality and replaced him with Brigadier Oswald Harker (who only lasted a year before being replaced by Sir David Petrie).

It was an inauspicious start for the security service and for many it felt as if the lessons of the First World War had been utterly forgotten.

Meanwhile, in Germany

The First World War brought German espionage crashing down. Kell's success against the enemy agents in Britain was just a part of it, and after the war Germany had to disband its secret service network – the only concession the Allies made was that the country could retain an intelligence unit for defensive purposes. This became the Abwehr in 1921, which frequently cropped up in interrogation reports as the usual source of enemy spies. However, when the Second World War broke out Hitler was already happily breaking the promise to the Allies of only having a 'defensive' intelligence network. Various organisations came into existence, such as the German Intelligence Service (GIS), the Nazi Security Service – Sicherheitsdienst (SD) – and the Reich Main Security Office – Reichssicherheitshauptamt (RSHA). These could easily fill several books in their own right.

But to understand the British interrogation story it is also necessary to understand some aspects of the enemy agencies it had to deal with. Whether it was through spies, refugees or POWs, time and time again the names of German security services cropped up and had to be understood by the interrogators if they were to be successful.

There was also the peculiar aspect of 'idea sharing' between the two systems. The most significant, and potentially the most damning to the British, was the escape and return to Berlin of POW Franz von Werra (his story was recorded in the book and film *The One That Got Away*). Von Werra had been through the whole interrogation system during his stay in Britain, and every trick in the book had been thrown at him without success – aside from a hidden microphone in his room that he failed to spot. On his return to Germany von Werra was attached to the intelligence division of the German air force and wrote a twelve-page pamphlet on his experiences as a POW and the various interrogation tricks used against him. Not only did this enable men to be briefed on what to expect if they were caught, but also how to outmanoeuvre the British. The ideas he listed were even incorporated into the interrogation tactics of Nazi intelligence, as they proved more successful than their own methods.

At the other end of the spectrum it was reported (and still remains a matter of controversy) that certain British interrogators had adopted Nazi methods, including physical torture. One intelligence officer, Professor Kennedy, would cause great controversy in the 1960s when it was rumoured that he had been involved in brainwashing POWs. But it is Lieutenant Colonel Scotland's name that regularly crops up in connection to such accusations. Complaints about him were numerous, the most significant being a long letter written by Fritz Knöchlein, an SS officer of the Totenkopf (Death's Head) Division, who was responsible for the massacre of around ninety POWs from the Royal Norfolk Regiment (see Chapter 7).

In his letter he quoted one interrogator at the London Cage saying to him: 'The Alexanderplatz in Berlin is not the only place where Gestapo methods existed. Here we can apply them much better … here we can smash you up much better … we'll smash you up miserably here. Here in this room you're going to be beaten so frightfully that you will whimper.'[8]

Knöchlein's actual experiences were fortunately the exception, with most British interrogators finding actual torture a pointless art, but playing on the idea of physical harm and inducing fear was a frequent tactic. The Germans' own interrogation system played into this game.

The mere word Gestapo is still enough to summon images of brutality and horror, but while time has faded the reality of those notions in modern minds, the soldiers and other prisoners coming into the hands of British interrogators would have a vivid picture of the work of their more dastardly comrades. The Gestapo, after 1939, came under the control of the Reich

Main Security Office (RSHA), run by Reinhard Heydrich, one of the most notorious Nazis of the war. He had also built up the SD, which now formed two sections for home intelligence and foreign intelligence. The Gestapo therefore became interlinked with the secret service and exploited its powers in interrogation.

There is no denying the horrors the Gestapo and associated authorities inflicted on Jews, subversives and POWs. Britons and Americans were not exempt from these treatments; their Prisoner of War status was usually signed off first, giving their captors unlimited scope for cruelties. Of Allied POWs in German hands, 28.6% witnessed and experienced torture and 57.1% suffered intimidation tactics. However, only 21.4% experienced an actual beating, while 50% stated they had witnessed beatings. (Compare this to Allied POWs in Japanese hands, where 71.4% suffered torture and 85.7% witnessed it.)[9]

Floggings, beatings, partial asphyxiation in cold water, electric currents attached to sensitive areas, crushing of male genitalia, hanging from the wrists until arms dislocated, burning and immersion in ice-cold water were just a few of the 'standard' procedures used. Despite the London Cage interrogator's boast that he could apply Gestapo methods far better, the complaints German prisoners made of the type of torture they experienced at British hands almost seem mild in comparison. There were similarities, however. Knöchlein talked of being regularly beaten and being forced into an ice-cold shower repeatedly until he became ill. Lieutenant Colonel Scotland was said to have told more than one prisoner that he had a hippopotamus whip he wanted to test out and regularly described a variety of tortures he could use on a man.

Knöchlein's story is compelling, but equally it can raise suspicions. He was, after all, an SS man on trial for his life based, in part, on his own confessions. The methods he described depicted Gestapo techniques he was no doubt deeply familiar with, and while Scotland undoubtedly used talk of torture to induce fear (a common enough tactic even in camps where torture was prohibited), whether this was put into practice remains in doubt.

On the other hand, Scotland's own denouncement of any physical abuse also sounds slightly hollow when it is known Lieutenant Colonel Stephens banned him from Camp 020 for hitting a recalcitrant suspect. There were also independent witnesses to prisoners being humiliated and forced to scrub floors with a guard casually kneeling on their back. So it seems some truth lies between the two accounts.

Undeniably Knöchlein's accounts, and even his experiences, were shaped by his knowledge of German torture techniques. Nazi propaganda at the start of the war made it clear that the British would indiscriminately torture any enemy they captured and most likely shoot them. Vilifying the enemy, however, only played into British hands and that fear could be exploited time and time again. It was also common practice to behave in a friendly and sympathetic way to new prisoners, alleviating their fears of brutality and generating such relief that the men almost eagerly talked to their new 'pals'.

Even after Franz von Werra exposed the fallacies of British torture, men still believed it and drove themselves into acute terror just by imagining what might happen to them. At Camp 020, Hendrik van Dam, who was proved innocent of spying, was thrown into such paroxysms of fear he began hallucinating that a woman was being tortured in a nearby cell and that he could hear her agonised screams (see Chapter 6). This was in fact a favourite game of the Gestapo, who would torture a woman in hearing distance of a male prisoner they wanted to break and often told him the terrible screams were that of his wife. Van Dam had no doubt heard of this practice from rumours, and when he realised his interrogators doubted his innocence, he tormented himself into delusions of horrendous torture being committed nearby.

Some Germans realised torture was an inadequate method of interrogation. Indeed, the Gestapo and other bodies employed it more for the sake of supposed expediency and to obtain confessions, caring less about the accuracy than about loosely incriminating more and more people.

A prime example is that of Wing Commander Forest Frederick Yeo-Thomas, a British subject who was raised and worked in France. During the Second World War he served as a British agent co-ordinating the various resistance movements in Europe in expectation of D-Day. His code name was 'Shelley', and he became somewhat of a legendary figure among the resistance in a short span of time – with the inevitable result that the Gestapo exerted a great deal of energy trying to catch him.

Yeo-Thomas was eventually betrayed, caught and immediately subjected to a vicious beating before being dumped before an interrogator. Stripped naked and beaten again, he was then questioned with limited results before being taken to a bathroom to be half-drowned in a tub of cold water and then artificially revived. Every time he came around he was asked the same question about the location of ammo dumps, and every time he feigned ignorance he was half-drowned again. In the first forty-eight hours in Gestapo hands, Yeo-Thomas spent considerably more time being tortured than he did answering questions. After a time he was so dazed by the abuse that he was only half-aware of what was going on and by that point he would have found answering any complex question, even if he wanted to, extremely difficult.

Forty-eight hours of torture and all the Gestapo learned was the name, rank and number of one of Yeo-Thomas' aliases – Kenneth Dodkin. British interrogators would have been disgusted by the failure. It was also obvious that the Gestapo only believed answers they wanted to hear. After further beatings, whippings and being suspended from his wrists from the ceiling until his shoulders nearly dislocated, Yeo-Thomas finally revealed a snippet of information. He gave the address of an apartment that one of the keys in his possession would unlock, content in the knowledge that having been missing for forty-eight hours, his colleagues would have abandoned the place.

The Germans rushed to the scene, but finding the place deserted they came to the conclusion that they had been hoodwinked and barely searched the place. Such was the ironic nature of much of their torturous interrogations that appeasing lies were believed and truths were tossed aside. Time and time again this was Yeo-Thomas' experience until it became clear that no answer would save him from pain, so where was the benefit in speaking any truth?

Modern studies of torture victims have only confirmed the negative psychological effects people experience under physical torment. Victims develop anxiety and depression, they tend to withdraw into themselves and become numbed to reality. From an interrogator's point of view, most disastrously, their intellectual abilities are actually impaired, resulting in difficulty in concentrating, confusion, memory loss and trouble following a line of questioning or similar conversation. Therefore torture can effectively ruin an interrogation.

These were Lieutenant Colonel Stephens' exact feelings on the use of torture – it only produced answers a prisoner thought their interrogator wanted to hear. There were so many risks involved; men who broke quickly under torture were unlikely to have any valuable knowledge, and the British were careful to pick agents who had the courage to stand up against pain and suffering. Also, it was a set rule that an agent was expected to reveal as little information as possible for the first forty-eight hours, giving time for his associates to disperse and go into hiding. Men were expected to eventually break under torture and, as this was understood, any agent that missed an appointment signalled a mass exodus of his colleagues to safe houses.

The threat of torture also induced intense fear and measures were taken to avoid it, such as standard-issue cyanide pills. When this failed, suspects would do anything to die quickly, saving themselves from pain and betraying their friends. Yeo-Thomas, after having his cyanide pill discovered, attempted to jump from a fourth-floor window to prevent the subsequent interrogation.

On the other hand, the British interrogators' more subtle means tended to lead agents into unwitting over-confidence, and this led them to relax and accidentally reveal information. In fact the closest Yeo-Thomas came to revealing any important information to his captives was when he was faced with an interrogator who just wanted to chat.

So why did the Germans resort to torture while the British refrained? In part it was the culture of the Gestapo and similar bodies. Men recruited for such divisions were expected to be brutal, unhesitatingly loyal to Hitler and prepared to do anything to their prisoners. Men were picked who enjoyed violence and who believed firmly in the Nazi mantra that they were superior to all others, especially Jews, Russians, partisans and French Resistance fighters. Extreme over-confidence led time and again to sneering disbelief in prisoners, which resulted in torture for predetermined answers.

A lack of intelligence backup also played a role. While British interrogators were constantly checking and double-checking the smallest piece of information, the Gestapo didn't have the same procedures and so missed vital details or were seriously duped. Yeo-Thomas witnessed this for himself when a man named Horace, who he believed was a traitor to the Resistance, was brought before him as the person who had given so much information on 'Shelley's' activities. Horace had told his Gestapo bosses that he was regularly talking to Shelley, who was currently in France inspecting ammo dumps, when in fact Yeo-Thomas had been back in Britain. His interrogators believed Horace emphatically and beat Yeo-Thomas for naming him a fraud, until he proved his charges.

Another vital factor was the lack of consequences. For many Gestapo men, since German victory was deemed inevitable, whom was there to fear reprisals from if they tortured, maimed and killed anybody they chose? Lack of consequences and unlimited power coupled with a brutal, immoral nature led to an inevitable reliance on torture.

For British interrogators it was a completely different story; not only were they aware that violent actions against prisoners could result in outcry from the public, the Red Cross and international authorities, but it could also lead to reprisals against British POWs in German hands. When the war ended and war criminals came under the auspices of the interrogators, another factor came into play – a man who was tortured for his confession could play on the story to a court and secure his freedom. A confession obtained under torture was utterly useless, because the international courts would doubt its credibility.

In fact, even the German military were aware of this and while the Gestapo have overshadowed German interrogation with their explicit use of violence, others were appalled by torture. The most famous example is Hanns Joachim Scharff, who served with Luftwaffe intelligence and regularly interrogated US airman. Opposed to violent persuasion he used the Luftwaffe's approved interrogation techniques, which largely involved becoming friendly with a prisoner and putting him at his ease. The exact same techniques, in fact, that Franz von Werra reported being used on him in England.

Initially a prisoner's fears of torture were played upon. Scharff tried to come across as wanting to help but if the prisoner didn't start talking and give basic details of name, rank and number then, as Scharff would apologetically say, he would have no option but to hand him over to the Gestapo as a suspected spy. On POWs this method was usually successful and once the early fear was over, Scharff worked on building a relationship with the prisoner, sharing meals and cigarettes, having discussions on politics and philosophy and even organising pleasure trips for his 'guests'. Prisoners often revealed information Scharff had been ordered to discover quite unwittingly.

Scharff kept detailed files on the various airmen who sat before him, and when faced with a particularly reluctant prisoner he would sift through his files and ask a question he already knew the answer to. He would explain that while he knew the information, his superiors wanted to hear it directly from the prisoner. Over the course of an interrogation session Scharff would keep asking questions and answering them from his notes in a bid to convince his prisoner that there was nothing he didn't already know about him. By the time he got to the one piece of information he didn't know, the prisoner would often volunteer it under the erroneous impression that Scharff already knew about it anyway. Scharff kept the Luftwaffe's actual lack of knowledge strictly secret to avoid ruining his trap. His methods could have found their mirror match in many British interrogation camps.

Scharff's methods, in contrast to those of his Gestapo brethren, were immensely successful despite his restraint (rumour has it he never even raised his voice to a prisoner). He became known as Nazi Germany's master interrogator, and when the war ended he was even invited to the US to explain his techniques so they might be used in training. Saved from the trials at Nuremburg because of his non-violent methods, he was one of the few Nazi interrogators who could come out of the war with praise.

He didn't have it all his own way though. Colonel Francis 'Gabby' Gabreski, America's top fighter ace, failed to be charmed by his methods and was one of the few who resisted revealing information. Despite that, the two men remained friends after the war.

Whether torture or talking, interrogation was still an infant product of the intelligence system and everyone was learning on their feet. Trial and error revealed what worked and what didn't, and with various authorities always looking over their shoulders the British interrogators learned to keep their cool under pressure. Their successes shortened the war and brought to light some of the worst atrocities of the conflict; they brought war criminals to their knees, uncovered top secret weapons, broke the German codes and rounded up spies, and it was mostly all done without raising a fist or even a voice.

Notes

1 Lieutenant Colonel Stephens (ed.), *A Digest of Ham, Volume One, A Digest of Ham on the Interrogation of Spies 1940–47.*

2 Sir Basil Thomson, *The Scene Changes*, Country Life Press, USA, 1937.

3 Ibid.

4 Lieutenant Colonel A.P. Scotland, *The London Cage*, Evans Brothers Ltd, 1957.

5 Ibid.

6 Ibid.

7 MI5 official history, *www.mi5.gov.uk/output/history.html.*

8 Fritz Knöchlein, *The London Cage: The Experiences of Fritz Knöchlein*, Steven Books, 2008.

9 Metin Basoglu (ed.), *Torture and its Consequences: Current Treatment Approaches*, Cambridge University Press.

2

MAKING A MAN TALK

What was the official process of interrogation? What procedures were followed? What protocol? What questions were asked and where? Who decided who was relevant and who was not?

The simple answer to all these logical questions is: it depends. In an age of pedantic paperwork, reams of red tape and an official procedure for even the minutiae of life, it can be hard to imagine how free-flowing and inconsistent the methods of interrogation in the Second World War were. Such vital work we would expect to have been governed by a series of rules and regulations, but there was little of the sort. The war interrogators had stepped into a new realm of defensive intelligence; never before had such vast numbers of soldiers, civilians and suspected spies been processed and there was hardly any guidance or precedent for the men responsible. It is fair to say that, to a reasonable extent, the interrogators made it up as they went along. Each interrogation centre had its own methods and there were more of these centres (usually separate from each other) than the official administration could properly deal with.

Individuals fell through the cracks, which is no surprise considering that the interrogators tended to form closed groups within their specific camp. In these groups men were trusted to follow the methods of the centre, usually laid down by a commandant, and there were unwritten rules and limitations, but also there was freedom to push boundaries and experiment within reason. The interrogators, working day in and day out with each other, grew familiar and even friendly. They came to rely and trust each other's words.

But there was also the element of secrecy. The information the British were drawing tenaciously from their prisoners was of vital importance to the war effort, sometimes concerning military manoeuvres or weapon development, sometimes discussing spy networks or double agents. This sort of information could not be talked about outside the walls of the interrogation centre, and interrogators themselves were not picked to be 'chatty'. A natural interrogator had to be a man who knew how to listen rather than talk – a man who kept close to his chest all he heard.

In such close-knit groups, the arrival of outsiders could cause tension, even when they were fellow interrogators. At Camp 020 it has already been mentioned that Lieutenant Colonel Stephens banned a fellow officer, Lieutenant Colonel Scotland, from ever interrogating one of his prisoners again after Scotland lost his temper with a man and hit him over the head. Scotland himself was paranoid about intrusions to his own camp and kept his doors firmly shut, even to the Red Cross. If admitting a stranger was unavoidable then efforts would be made to remove anything deemed 'highly confidential' (or in some cases 'highly controversial'). The worst dread was an outsider gaining official permission to interview a prisoner alone, making it impossible for the 'house' interrogators to know what passed between them – unless of course you were Lieutenant Colonel Stephens and hid microphones in interview rooms.

Secretive, private and suspicious of intrusion, officially governing the interrogators was far from easy – nor was it of high priority. So the interrogation centres operated on their own methods, own morals even, and their styles were as diverse as their views on the men in their charge.

A Time and Place

Interrogation of a prisoner could happen in a number of locations. From the instant an enemy was captured he was assailed with questions. British officers on the front line formed the first interrogators, getting the basic information from a POW before passing him on. Often these men were of surprising significance. If they captured a man it was up to them to decide if he was a lower-ranked soldier or someone of greater importance. More than one Nazi attempted to escape detection by pretending to be a low-ranking military man or a civilian. If their ruse was successful then they would be shipped to an ordinary holding camp along with other mundane POWs, thus vital time would be lost and information could lose its value if the prisoner was unidentified for too long.

The interrogators, in part, had to rely on their colleagues on the battle-field to supply them with the correct men. Similarly, back on British shores, the police and other defensive bodies (such as the Home Guard) provided another early interrogation system. They were responsible for not only cap-turing escaped prisoners, but for identifying and capturing suspected spies. While MI5 had its own intelligence network for locating enemy agents, they needed the widespread eyes of the police to catch them. On one of his sojourns from camp, Franz von Werra, the most famous of POW escapees, found himself confronted with detectives from the Criminal Investigation Department (CID). He was afraid they had come to arrest him, instead, they had come to confirm the story he had been spreading that he was a crashed Dutch pilot fighting for the Allies in a special operations unit. Much to his delight the CID men believed him and left him a free man.

Fortunately for the British, on this occasion at least, von Werra's story was not believed by the RAF, who had also been informed about the 'Dutch pilot' and who sent a car to pick him up so they could test his claims. Von Werra would later end up back in a prison camp, but his story illustrates how the skills of the police could be just as essential to the interrogators as the skills of their own men.

Prisoners captured abroad went through a process of holding camps, termed 'cages', where interrogation was minimal unless they were rec-ognised as important figures. As soon as was possible they were delivered to England where their first sight would often be the infamous Tower of London. The place they were destined for was little better than the dreaded medieval castle.

The London Cage – initially another processing point for all prisoners – quickly became exclusive to those more dangerous or informative indi-viduals. Ordinary POWs would be roughly processed and sent on to various camps across the country; those deemed important found themselves at the London Cage, a glamorous mansion that hid a wealth of secrets (see

Chapter 7). This was the headquarters of Lieutenant Colonel Scotland, who would later become known for his 'interviews' of suspected war criminals.

Scotland worked on a process of humiliation and contempt. Reluctant prisoners were penalised by being embarrassed before other men, forced to do endless menial tasks, and psychologically abused. He was later accused of torture, but that will be discussed further on. Scotland's methods were extreme, and were criticised by his contemporaries, but despite that no one officially intervened and Scotland was allowed to continue with his unorthodox methods.

At the other end of the spectrum was Lieutenant Colonel Stephens ('Tin Eye' Stephens as he was affectionately known). No man could be more different from Scotland. Stephens presented the image of a typical interrogator; in fact, remove his British insignia and you could easily imagine him as the stereotypical 1940s spy. With his dark hair swept back and closely shaved at the sides, a monocle wedged in his right eye and the bearing of a fierce and determined man, he looked like someone a German spy would not want to cross swords with.

He was a complete contrast to the meek-looking Scotland, who had the appearance of a quintessential rural squire, with his round glasses, white hair and grandfatherly look. Out of the two it would be easy to suppose that Stephens was the one prone to dark methods of interrogation instead of the cosy-looking Scotland. The opposite was the case. No one abhorred the use of extreme methods more than Stephens, not from any great sympathy for his captives, but because he considered it a lazy man's option and one prone to forcing untruthful answers to please an interrogator.

Stephens was the commandant of Camp 020 and the author of *A Digest of Ham*, one of the few documents that gives a first-hand account of how an interrogator went about his business. Camp 020 was situated near Ham Common, in the London Borough of Richmond, not that far from his nemesis Scotland (Stephens made no pretence of hiding that he detested the man). But his remit for Camp 020 was far different from the war criminals being tried at the London Cage. Stephens dealt virtually exclusively with suspected spies, most of who were not German or were unconnected with the military. They were seemingly ordinary men and women, ranging from businessmen to journalists, to rich playboys and prostitutes. A few married couples even came through his doors. For most visitors to

Camp 020 there were only two possible fates – execution or becoming a double agent. Stephens' system, the Double-Cross System, relied extensively on his work. He not only interviewed spies, but selected suitable candidates for the scheme, sending any man he deemed unreliable to a quick appointment with the firing squad or hangman.

For general prisoners of war there were several places set aside for CSDIC (Combined Services Detailed Interrogation Centre) interrogators in both the UK and Europe. They would continue their work long after the war, their most notorious centre being Bad Nenndorf CSDIC camp in Germany. These camps processed a range of men, dealing with numerous topics from morale to the latest German armaments, and the vast majority of prisoners would have had their interrogation conducted by a CSDIC man. The extensive interrogation reports that still exist show a rambling series of conversations held between German prisoners and British interrogators. Sometimes they were condensed into more readable reports, and not only do they expose the military mentality of the Germans but also open a window into that troubled time.

Prisoners might also experience less formal interrogations, whether that was from officers visiting the camp or from policemen interviewing them if they were suspected in a crime. For the most part, interrogators were under the auspices of MI5 and doing work on their behalf, but internal controls were another matter, depending mostly on the camp commandant and his preferences. At a time when Germany seemed the greatest threat to the British nation, the interrogators were gladly left to their own devices as long as they achieved results.

Forms and Red Tape

Early attempts to sort through refugees arriving in droves from Europe for potential enemy spies had been chaotic and rather informal. Examiners at a port of entry would assess newcomers by running a finger down a list to see if any of the names rang a bell. Ultimately it was a useless system and very rapidly it was arranged that any prisoner who could not provide immediate and unequivocal identification would be sent to a single holding area to be processed. After reorganisation in 1942 this site became the LRC (London

Reception Centre) and was the starting point for many enemy agents and collaborators to enter the British interrogation system.

The LRC took the collecting of information seriously and built up an extensive card-index scheme to help identify true refugees from agents. The Abwehr were particularly fond of using the 'refugee route': planting a spy or two in a group of genuine immigrants to get them safely into England. The LRC's role was not just to detect spies but to quickly deal with innocent suspects; their database assisted with this by providing everything from the known routes and methods of German agents, to the genuine routes used by Allied resistance movements.

The LRC became so successful at screening enemy agents from among real refugees that Germany started to brief its spies on the reception centre and prepare them for interview, but the extensive information index held by the LRC made it increasingly difficult to create a convincing cover story for spies. Out of around 33,000 aliens that came through the LRC only three enemy agents avoided detection; it was a tremendous success.

At this early stage of interrogation the atmosphere was friendly and relaxed, and this was largely due to the LRC staff recognising that 95% of the people in their charge were innocent of any crime and had, indeed, suffered greatly before arriving in England. Individual interviews were conducted on a one-to-one basis, while large groups of prisoners brought in en masse had the pleasure of filling in questionnaires to save time.

Britain is occasionally accused of its red tape obsession, its love of paperwork and the accompanying rigmarole, and the LRC gave credit to this claim; after all the first thing a newly arrived refugee in England could expect was a short questionnaire.

POWs had similar experiences. Franz von Werra was confronted with a form helpfully printed in English and German that he likened in his memoirs to a hotel guest register. It asked for the usual details of name, rank and number, and then went on to more probing questions such as home address, unit, army post office number and the nature of the prisoner's mission when he crashed in England. Von Werra deliberately left those boxes empty, but even he had to wonder how many of his comrades had fallen for a similar tactic. It seems too simple that a form could have extracted vital information from a man, but it was the case and no doubt many men were judged for further questioning based on their answers, or lack of.

Depending on the nature of the suspect, whether he was a POW or a possible spy, he would find himself (or herself, in some cases) following one of two routes. A military prisoner was shipped to one of the many POW camps springing up across the UK, and any further interrogation might happen there or at a CSDIC base.

A suspected agent, however, found themselves on a short trip to Camp 020, where there was one issue in mind – proving their guilt or innocence, and then extracting as much information as possible. The two routes varied in one other significant factor: the POWs were merely playing with information – their knowledge of war – but the spies were gambling with their lives. Proving beyond doubt that a man was a spy was a new endeavour for the secret service and there were no precedents to help them along; only their own mixture of ad hoc rules and trial-and-error processes.

Wherever they arrived, the POWs or spies were usually initiated into camp life with a strip search and medical examination. The officers were looking for anything from hidden weapons or documents to secret ink concealed in false teeth, as well as the spy's favourite, the cyanide pill. For enemy agents it was common to take a photograph, both for use in future interviews with other suspects and also in case of escape; POWs were too numerous for the same process to apply to them.

Once searched and examined the prisoners were issued with typical POW clothing, which would have some form of insignia prominently placed on it to indicate that the man was a British captive. Once everything was settled the suspected spies were taken to a cell inside the interrogation camps, usually for solitary confinement. The same procedure was sometimes carried out with POWs who were thought to hold useful details.

The Right Man for the Job

'The difficulty of setting out the requirements for a first class interrogator is more apparent than real. In theory, remarkable attainments are essential. In practice an average officer is posted and the best use is made of his limited qualification, enthusiasm and experience.'[1] Said the formidable and dry-witted Lieutenant Colonel Stephens. Interrogators were simply not that easy to find; there was no real record kept of men from the First World War who had served such a function and might be pressed back into service, and many of those men were too old (or dead) for the role. When in his 60s, Lieutenant Colonel Scotland was an exception when he was drafted back in due to his First World War experience, but in general men had to be found through more surreptitious routes.

The most common method was via private channels and personal recommendation, but what qualities were they looking for? Proficiency in languages seemed an obvious choice, experience of life and the world through travel was another qualification that at least could be assessed, but less easy to judge was the ability to be adaptable and quick-witted. Interrogators needed to be able to change tactics with a suspect at a moment's notice, but not everyone was capable of such a feat, nor were they sharp enough to pick up on erroneous comments or errors in the prisoner's story. Many men were put forward for the work and many were turned down.

Stephens was as critical of would-be interrogators as he was about the spies in his charge. He firmly believed that there were only two types of interrogator – the Breaker and the Investigator. The Breaker had an obvious role: he had to go in fast and 'break' a man, confirm his guilt and get him to write out a full confession.

'[The Breaker] is a paragon, so to say, who is expected to overwhelm and disintegrate all opposition.'[2]

Stephens put himself firmly in this bracket, making the role of the Breaker almost into a legendary figure. He was philosophical in his thoughts on the matter: 'It is customary to say a breaker is born and not made. Perhaps the first class breaker has yet to be born. Perhaps he has yet to be recruited from the concentration camps, where he has suffered for years, where, above all he has watched and learnt in bitterness every move in the game.'

Above all else, Stephens believed, 'there must be an implacable hatred of the enemy'. It was a grim analogy – the bitter victim turned against his tormentors, lacking sympathy, detesting the suspect, remote from their suffering. This bleak outline of a man, which Stephens fitted to himself, is one of the few times his truly dark side emerges in his words. A dark side we shall return to later.

The Breaker had to be a natural cynic, who took everything his subject said with a degree of scepticism, and he needed patience (sometimes extreme patience) to pursue a man until he finally caved. Doggedness, determination and a driven temperament, no matter the impossible odds thrown at him, were all key traits: '… the Breaker should confine his undivided attention to the spy, the relentless pursuit of his plan, and indeed leave interpretation, the taking of notes, and the custody of property to others.'

There were those, however, who felt the Breaker was a disagreeable role and not necessary when prisoners were treated courteously. One young officer in Stephens' division had recently come out of training and was more inclined to use an academic approach against suspects. He firmly disapproved of 'breaks'. With this in mind, he set about interviewing a spy by first collecting his facts and setting out a list of 300 questions that he wanted answers to. Upon meeting his suspect he took the stance of 'giving him the benefit of the doubt' and helpfully outlined the case against the man. He showed him the list of questions he hoped he would answer and then asked him politely what his response was.

With equal politeness the spy replied that he was not the man the interrogator was looking for. Knocked from his stride, the young officer foolishly then stated that he supposed none of his questions would apply. The spy apologetically answered that that was the case.

Convinced by this game, the officer reported that they had the wrong man in the cells and that it was a terrible case of mistaken identity. Stephens' fury at this statement can only be imagined; another man was set on the task, but the spy had been given the upper hand. He knew the case against him and the gaps in the interrogators' knowledge. He took many hours of interviews to break and even so it was not a complete break. It can only be assumed that the young officer was kicked out of Camp 020 with a large flea in his ear.

After the Breaker came the less intimidating Investigator, whose role it was to gather as much information as possible from the defeated spy. In contrast to his counterpart he did not require the same tenacity and dispassion; in fact a slightly sympathetic ear could prove useful after the onslaught of the Breaker, but he still needed to be a man the subject would respect and respond to. In this respect Stephens also had an opinion – he considered the man who in civilian life was a barrister to be a failure as an interrogator: 'Maybe something is wanting in his attack. Not unexpectedly he regards the case as an intellectual foray. He feels bound by the ethics of his profession.

He depends upon his brief.' In short, such a man was too tight-laced and restricted by need for papers and legal justification. He needed to reverse his thinking – every spy was guilty until proven innocent.

The man Stephens was looking for had a broad interest in diverse topics, which enabled him to talk sensibly with his suspect on whatever subject came up. If the spy talked ships he needed an interrogator who could respond appropriately; if he talked about desert warfare he needed a man who understood fighting in a hot climate – he needed someone he could talk to, as simple as that. Even so, every suspect was different. Some would not respond to a young man, however well educated on his subject or enthusiastic he was. Some would not respond to a 'playboy' type or would be resentful of a well-spoken, obviously wealthy interrogator. So much depended on the personality of the individual, upon his mood and upon his motives. Picking the right interrogator for the job was more than just choosing a man who spoke the language – he had to be compatible with his interviewee, and if they got it wrong, then an interrogator was expected to be prepared to withdraw ('without jealousy') and allow another man to take his place.

There was no room for an interrogator who was precious, prone to being closed and secretive about his work and obsessed by his own self-importance. He was a danger to the whole system that relied on teamwork and a level of trust difficult to find outside the interrogation centre. All interrogators worked to a 'plan', a rough outline of the objectives of an interview and how to go about achieving them; there was room for flexibility, but outright changes were the responsibility of the commandant alone. Most commandants, in fact, were very hands on in their approach to interrogation and liked to be part of every interview where feasible. Critical interviews of important prisoners were deemed the responsibility of the commandant alone.

That was another piece of the puzzle the British learned. It was best for the interrogator to always outrank the prisoner who was being interviewed, even if this was not his normal ranking. Senior officer POWs responded best to a full colonel, while the more arrogant German generals were best dealt with by an interrogator who experienced a temporary elevation to the peerage.

Another vital person among the interrogators was a psychiatrist, not that he was readily accepted or even respected by the men around him. At Camp 020 this was Dr Harold Dearden, also known for his passion for writing.

Dearden was regularly at loggerheads with Stephens over prisoner treatment and the two men argued so violently in 1943 that Dearden threatened to resign. It was one of the rare instances that Stephens reluctantly apologised, though he later remarked in his book: 'Strange people psychiatrists; even in war.'

In fact, from *A Digest of Ham* it could almost seem that there was no psychiatrist at the camp. Dearden was virtually (and tellingly) written out of the history by Stephens, despite often sitting in on interrogations and providing his own thoughts on a suspect.

Double agent Tate met Dearden first-hand when he arrived at Camp 020 after parachuting into the Fens. Tate's real name was Schmidt and he had been caught out in Cambridge by the local police who thought the very English sounding name of Harry Johnson appearing in his passport was at odds with the man's strong accent.

Schmidt arrived at Camp 020 on 21 September 1940 and entered a room where two army officers and the psychiatrist, Dearden, were awaiting him. 'I was fascinated by the strange old man [Dearden] in civilian clothes. He was reading a newspaper. He looked at me briefly as I came in then went on reading. I couldn't take my eyes off him.'[3]

Dearden had cross-examined criminals in his civilian career and now used tactics his fellow interrogators would have approved of to become a quiet, yet observant participant in the interviews of spies.

Despite Dearden's presence, Schmidt was not about to crack easily. He maintained a story before his interrogators that he had been in England since July and had not parachuted in, but had been delivered by a Danish fishing boat – a slightly less suspicious entry. He claimed he had arrived in the north and travelled southwards along the coast living on cake and chocolate, aiming to eventually arrive at the Danish consul in London. Lieutenant Colonel Stephens was exacerbated by this fictitious story and determined to reveal it for the lie it was. In one excerpt from the interrogations he demanded:

[Stephens] Who cut your hair last?
[Schmidt] I did not cut it.
[St] You have not had your hair cut for two and a half months?
[Sc] Yes. When I came it was very short.

[St] How much longer are you going on with this nonsense? Do you know what a man looks like whose hair has been growing for two and a half months?

[Sc] It is different. My beard does not grow either.

[St] How often did you shave?

[Sc] Three days or four days.

[St] What did you shave with?

[Sc] I have this knife and these blades.

[St] What laundry did you go to on the way? Which shop washed your clothes?

[Sc] When I came I had two shirts more and socks. This is the last of those I brought.

[St] It looks as if you have been marching all this distance with dirty clothes.

[Sc] I had more clothes and I threw them away.[4]

Stephens' frustration can be felt as he tried to break the elusive Schmidt, whose story was so laughable that it beggars belief that he could stick to it without laughing. He did eventually recant his bogus cover story and admit that he had been parachuted in recently, though he had a vague feeling he had landed in the wrong place. Dearden now laid his thoughts on the table about the suspect; he had noticed that Schmidt was deeply confused about the condition of England and its people.

Schmidt had landed in 1940 at a time when Germany was confidently proclaiming that the invasion of Britain was imminent. He had read and heard the propaganda, the inflated damage figures being touted, the news about the disintegrating morale of the English and the devastation the Luftwaffe had caused. Yet, when he had arrived in the Fens he discovered people going about their everyday lives and the signs of war, and certainly war damage, were minimal.

On route to Camp 020 his driver had made the cunning decision to pass by Whitehall, the Houses of Parliament and Westminster Abbey, so that Schmidt could see how incredible the Nazi lies were. Even before he arrived at the interrogation centre Schmidt was feeling deeply disheartened and conscious that he had been extensively lied to by his masters. Dearden recognised that this disillusionment had led to the depression of Schmidt's spirits and that exploiting it could be the key to turning him.

He also laid store in the man's sense of humour, even under interrogation. 'If we all wait a short while longer,' Schmidt said during one interview, 'you will all be my prisoners.'[5] Both these factors, he believed, were worth using to press the man into British service. When he mentioned his ideas to one of the interrogators, they instantly concurred and laughingly said Schmidt reminded them of the music hall comedian Harry Tate – Tate would eventually become Schmidt's double agent code name.

When Schmidt did eventually crack, this was partly due to the British playing on the Nazis' deception and also to the invisible threat of the hangman's noose looming in his mind. Schmidt turned and became a successful double agent, so trusted by the Germans that he eventually became an appointed paymaster and contact for future agents, leading them straight into their doom. He was even awarded two Iron Crosses for his service. Yet Dearden's reports and the influence they had on transforming Schmidt into Tate are completely missing from Stephens' history of the camp. Perhaps no greater evidence is needed to show how the interrogators chose to distance themselves from the psychiatrist in their midst. Psychiatrists were a valuable asset to most interrogation centres, yet to the minds of some interrogators they were crackpot nuisances who really didn't know what they were talking about. No wonder they have been almost excised from the interrogation records.

Processing People

All interrogations had to start with an objective and that was a simple one: 'Truth in the shortest possible time.'[6] Whether the man in question was a potential spy, a traitor or merely a POW with useful information, the process was the same. Information was needed and fast. A little motto of Stephens' that was (and still is) immensely appropriate, went: 'Some information in time is worth more than an encyclopaedia out of date.' There was no greater demand on an interrogator than the need for the right information at the right time, and this pressing deadline always hanging over a man's head could lead some to falter and use threats and violence to get their way.

A good interrogator would never be driven to fall in such a style, however. They worked consistently and patiently, and often the end result – the report laid on an officer's desk – seemed sparse compared to the time it had taken to extract the information. When a conversation was whittled down to its objective core, it could often end with a bullet point defining an hour of talk. The ultimate goal when dealing with an enemy agent or presumed traitor was a confession, signed, sealed and irrefutable; something to be held over the suspect at future interviews and to be referred to when he tried to retract a statement or lie. In some of the files, preliminary reports (usually confessions) were typed onto yellow paper to make them easy to find when sorting through a stack of documents. These lemon-shaded pages became dubbed the 'yellow perils' since they often led to the doom of an agent. He was effectively caught, tried and ready for execution once his story hit the yellow pages. An example of what a yellow peril would look like and contain can be seen in the preliminary report on the man Copier:

'Copier is pro-German, to this day a fanatic, and certainly proud of his conduct. His glory, in his esteem, is his faith. His undoing is the obstinacy of a weak man, for he is unable to see he is a traitor to Holland. His tragedy is myopia; indeed, for practical purposes, in a fast moving world, he is blind. He must peer for enlightenment, but even this has become a heel-clicking drill … he was rejected for the Waffen SS Service then became a gnawing obsession even to the point of envy when a soldier came back without an arm … he talks of "honest National Socialism" which is a contradiction in terms.'[7]

This yellow peril reads more like an extract from a novel than a straightforward report, but placing a man emotionally was an important part of the interrogator's role. Mere facts of where, what and how were useful but failed to bring alive the character of the person, and if an interrogator had to remove himself from a case, his replacement had to be able to get inside the suspect's head immediately. Therefore, presenting a story to bring the man alive and define his personality, his weaknesses and motives was just as necessary as laying out how he arrived in England and what his mission was. Psychologically analysing a spy was also the only way to determine whether he would be any use for 'turning' – the Double-Cross System being a fundamental aspect of British wartime espionage.

The yellow peril also could list the details of a suspect's activities for easy reference. Career, training, names of fellow agents, code names and dates of missions would all be recorded and kept for future reference. At any point, if a suspect came into an interrogation centre whose name rang a bell, then the case officers could go through their files to discover if there was anything there they could use against him, and more than once this was the case.

How the prisoner was treated in these early stages of the interview depended on the centre and what he was being interrogated for. Among POWs, where numbers were too high to enable strict and efficient separation of useful and non-useful men, a subject often remained with his comrades before being called for an interview. Sometimes this did not matter, especially if the topics of interest were technical matters, but in cases were a military manoeuvre or a Nazi travesty were in question, then leaving the men together would only enable them to compare notes and develop a 'party line'. This was a serious concern when the rounding up of major war criminals began on the cessation of hostilities. Strict solitary confinement and no talking was enforced, even when the men came together to exercise. The less information that could be shared between them, the more likely the interrogators could achieve a satisfactory result.

The same applied to supposed spies – even communication with the guards was kept to a minimum. The suspect was to be arrested quietly and quickly, searched and assigned prison garb as soon as possible, and to be kept in virtual silence. The idea was to produce a feeling of depression and despair in the victim. He should feel no compassion, no hope from his guards. They should not respond to any question, unless it was essential and about their duties. No information was to be imparted and there were to be, 'No exceptions. No chivalry. No gossip. No cigarettes.'

It was hoped that the end result would produce a man so relieved to be talking with another human being that he would open up unwittingly to an interrogator. It certainly had an effect in many cases at Nuremberg where such strict procedures were the norm.

As soon as the prisoner was settled his belongings were sorted through for anything useful. Amazingly, large numbers of prisoners came to Britain with incriminating or highly sensitive documents on their person. For early Luftwaffe pilots this was simply because they believed the war would end so soon that anything they carried would be useless to their captors. Others kept notes, and snippets of paper as memory aids, sometimes loosely coding them, but never sufficiently to elude a keen interrogator for long. The wealth of knowledge the intelligence services could obtain in this way was startling, and the failing was not exclusive to the Germans and their agents.

The British agent Yeo-Thomas reported with fury that the new heads of the Resistance units in France kept detailed and highly dangerous records of their workings and agents. When he pointed out the risk he was laughed off – ultimately the records were captured by the Nazis and several of these leaders went to their deaths due to the documents they insisted on keeping.

The first interview of a prisoner was the most significant; it set the tone for what would follow and a bad first round could ruin the chances of getting a prisoner to talk. Stephens liked the atmosphere of this first interview to be similar to that of a general court martial. One officer would conduct the interrogation and was not to be interrupted for any reason. In urgent cases, summaries of the interview were recorded at the same time as it was being conducted by officers who took it in shifts to write their observations in an adjoining office. The aim was to have a quick report ready for inspection by a senior officer within an hour of the interrogation ending, rather than having to wait for one.

If necessary, there was an interpreter present; this was more common than not as most interrogators had limited foreign language skills. Finding these interpreters was a task in itself, and at the Nuremberg interrogations there was a severe shortage from the Allied side. In the end, Germans with a good grasp of English had to be drafted in. Unless the room was rigged for microphones there was also a stenographer who was surreptitiously relieved every half hour.

Prisoners were marched into the room and expected to stand to attention during the interview – another means of lowering morale – and the interview remained strictly formal; there was little room for abstract conversations or 'chattiness'. Stephens disliked the method some of his colleagues used of inducing familiarity with a suspect as he felt it bred confidence in the spy and reduced the chances of a break. He was probably right.

It was a very different approach to that metered out to Franz von Werra. He went through the more 'traditional' process. His first interview was with a gentlemanly officer who offered him a cigarette and expressed no interest in the interrogation, but would rather like to talk about Germany. His whole stance was designed to lull the suspect into a false sense of security, get him chatting, relax him and hopefully have him divulge something useful. It was tactic often used to great effect against ordinary POWs – men who weren't lying for their lives and had nothing much to lose by 'having a chat'.

The gist of the matter is that depending on the suspect and depending on the interrogator the style of interview varied greatly. There was no fixed method and some men experienced more than one version of an interview. Franz von Werra eventually found himself in a stricter interrogation with the cliché of a light shining in his face, but that was after he had outwitted his first jovial interrogator. By this point the game was over – he was not about to break.

So what was an actual interrogation like? It had its formula, as all procedures do. The first was to establish confidently who they were dealing with – which unit, which rank, if a military man or real name, aliases and masters worked for, if a suspected spy, etc. Even this could be a challenge, as some men chose to lie while others played dumb, and the interrogators used tricks such as putting two men together who they thought were in the same unit and seeing how they reacted. They also delved regularly into their detailed files to help them piece together the puzzle (see Chapter 3).

The interrogation had to be quick-fire. Questions were fired at the suspect and any information of significance the prisoner revealed had to be written down to avoid retraction later. Stephens liked the term, 'blow hot, blow cold'. No respite was given and interviews came at all times, day and night. Session lengths varied and the prisoner was given little time to rest and regain his thoughts; in short, the prisoner was expected to suffer mental torture. The strain on both sides was immense, but necessary: if a vital suspect did not break in those first few sessions there was a risk he would not break at all and every interrogator was aware of this very real danger.

Yet there was one thing Stephens was adamant about: 'Never strike a man. For one thing it is the act of a coward. For another, it is unintelligent, for the spy will give an answer to please, an answer to escape punishment. And having given a false answer, all else depends upon the false premise.'

If only all interrogators had taken this stance, Britain's interrogation war record would have remained untainted by controversies over torture and Gestapo methods in London.

Methods of Madness

There were various devices and styles the interrogators could employ to succeed in breaking a man, some will be dealt with more fully in later chapters, but a few are worth covering here. The most logical of tactics is direct confrontation; facing a man with another who knows him and can tell about his activities seems an almost foolproof way to break down his defences. But it was not the case when a man was determined to stick to his cover. Prisoners would blandly deny all knowledge of their best friend if they feared acknowledging him would reveal more than they wanted to.

Confrontation could drastically backfire, as in the case of the two spies Verlinden and Laureyssens. Verlinden was a reliable British informant who had actually introduced Laureyssens to his German spy master. He had provided accommodation for him and knew all about his mission details, he could even explain how Laureyssens earned his keep in Lisbon by accurately locating for his masters British targets and AA defences in Swansea. With all this evidence it seemed impossible that Laureyssens could not talk. He was presented with what was almost his life history and calmly denied all of it.

Frustrated, the interrogators chose to confront him directly with Verlinden, convinced that seeing the man could not help but force him to speak. Verlinden was brought into the room and retold his story before his comrade. As he finished speaking Laureyssens looked at him without a flicker of emotion and calmly denied all knowledge of him, too.

It was a situation that occurred far too often, especially with agents or high-ranking military men determined to keep their secrets. Confrontation became an altogether risky business, yet it was still resorted to when a suspect had otherwise eluded questioning.

A similar version of this tactic was the 'cross-ruff' – playing two men off against each other. It worked best against prisoners who worked closely together and shared a cover story; this could be two spies or Nazi officers trying to cover up a war crime. The men were separated and initial interviews determined who appeared to be the weaker of the two. This weaker individual would then be subjected to heavy and continuous interrogation until he broke down. A successful break was then turned into a written statement, and the transcript was taken and presented to the broken individual's comrade. It was rare that the second didn't recognise that the game was up and that any further lies would do him more harm than good.

A significant example of the cross-ruff was that of the Icelandic agents Fresenius, Bjornsson and Juliusson. Within the trio Fresenius was the commander and the other two were little more than his servants following

orders. As soon as they were captured they were divided up and the interrogators set to work, initially on Bjornsson. It did not take long for them to
achieve a partial break, which they then used immediately against Juliusson.
Juliusson also supplied a limited confession, which was played back against
Bjornsson and, through a series of back and forth interviews, the whole
story, mission and case against Fresenius was obtained. Fresenius was now in
hot water. At his first interrogation he was presented with a complete case
history of his crimes, and in the end he really had no option but to concede
the truth. The remarkable aspect about this case was that it came at the time
of D-Day and the information was successfully collected within forty-eight
hours – it must have been one of those impressive cross-ruffs of the war.

The most melodramatic and theatrical of methods employed by the
interrogators was the 'assessors'. Devised at Camp 020, it was a deliberately farcical performance that had its origins in a memory of pre-war Italy,
where patrons of a pavement cafe would argue the hours away over some
point of illogical logic. The idea was simple – confront a man with his fellows and ask them to advise, comment and argue with him.

The assessors were fellow inmates; as the idea was developed at Camp
020, this made them spies. Some were men who had broken and revealed
all and were hopeful for their freedom, others had persisted in lying and
were now purely awaiting their executions. However, they had one aspect
in common: all their cases were finished with. They had no more use to the
interrogators and were freely available for the scam.

The assessors were brought into a room and politely offered seats; they
were then told they would be presented with a fellow countryman. His
case would be presented to them and they were to consider it. During the
interview of the prisoner they would be needed to assist, to advise and to
help their comrade. It sounds peculiar, perhaps even counter-productive,
but in Stephens' words:

'Sometimes it works like a charm. The unbroken spy is marched in. Alone
he stands. When he makes a ridiculous reply, reference is made to his countrymen. They are invited to give an opinion. When the spy loses his temper,
they are invited to calm him. When they side with their countryman they
are reminded they are doing themselves no good. When they side against
him they are told there may be hope at least for their families to work again
in peace in the vineyards, to sing again under a moonlit sky.'

Stephens had his poetic moments, but the principal was sound and occasionally it had unexpected results. In one case the suspect failed to respond to the assessors, but ironically one of these phoney court men broke instead and offered a full confession.

A favourite method, which was used quite widely on reluctant prisoners, was to 'blow hot, blow cold' or, in modern terms, 'good cop, bad cop'. The principal of the scheme, to scare the suspect and then present him with a sympathetic ear, has not diminished with time if played well. The game was particularly effective against the conceited prisoner, or one who believed his standing would protect him from rough interrogation. This could be the traitorous diplomat, or the arrogant Nazi convinced Hitler would be coming for him soon.

The first step was to knock the man down a peg or two. The usual procedures of removing their clothes and replacing them with prison garb began the process, followed by relieving the prisoner of anything that could potentially pose a suicide risk (pince-nez, false teeth, bootlaces). The humanitarian point was stretched considerably to achieve the result (though it could be supposed that a desperate man could choke himself to death on his own false teeth). There was nothing more demeaning to a person then reducing them to a shuffling figure unable to speak properly or see clearly, and it was all in the name of human concern. Those standing trial at Nuremberg spent weeks without bootlaces, shuffling pathetically around the exercise yard and down the corridors.

Once this personal humiliation was achieved the prisoner was ready for the next step and was brought before an interrogation board. One officer, usually the commandant, verbally assaulted the prisoner with a withering report on his activities, with one or two unimportant errors added in to make it seem convincing. The commandant made himself out to be a bully; he would appear to get so caught up in his intense rage at a traitor that he would shout and scream at a prisoner without allowing him a chance to defend himself. At one point another officer would try to intervene and would be violently reproached for doing so. The suspect was then abruptly dismissed, all without being able to say a word.

Back at his cell it was hoped the prisoner would be feeling both outraged and shaken, no doubt wondering what the next step would be and whether he would actually get a chance to speak up for himself. Apparently by pure coincidence, the orderly officer of the day would turn out to be the man who tried to intercede for the forlorn prisoner at the interrogation. He would come across as polite and sympathetic to the suspect's plight, he might even explain that the commandant was an unreasonable man, ferocious with all supposed traitors and not inclined to treat a sensitive man with any consideration. Almost sorrowfully he would explain the case against the suspect was conclusive and the commandant was determined to get the last few details and be done with it.

The commandant was always painted as such a hard and merciless interrogator that the following interviews were likely to be extremely difficult for the suspect. The officer then offered to smooth the way to a more dignified approach. If only the suspect would write a clear statement, a sort of confession, it would be bound to help him avoid another vile performance by the commandant against him. Perhaps it would even spare his family from potential blackmail? The play-off usually had the desired effect once the suspect had had a chance to sleep on it. Very often he would even happily talk of the orderly officer who had so hoodwinked him as an outstanding gentleman, while the commandant was spoken of as if he was the head of the Gestapo. There was another bonus to this deception. The suspect might spread talk of the volatile commandant among his comrades and make them more receptive to the same treatment.

Similar to this was the use of 'sympathy men', though this ploy was not as popular an interrogation tool for the British as it was for the Germans. They usually came in the guise of welfare officers and got chummy with the POWs by feeling empathy for their situation. A popular deception was to pretend to have been a POW in the First World War so they could appear to understand what the prisoner was going through. They would provide little treats, such as cigarettes, to their new friends, supposedly against camp regulations, and little by little they came to be known as a 'good sort' who could be trusted.

Once they were accepted they started to probe for information, very subtly at first, pretending they were completely ignorant about a topic such as U-boats or coding and asking pointless questions. As time went by their questions would gradually improve until they felt confident they could get an answer to a very specific question on a technical matter that the interrogators had failed to uncover. At other times they would simply plant the seed of an idea in the prisoner's mind and hope that when he was back in his room with other men he would talk about it for the benefit of a hidden microphone.

In the same way, an army officer would be sent to escort German air force or navy prisoners when they were going out to work or exercise. It was felt that these men might be more willing to talk freely with an officer of a different branch of the service to their own – again the officer would feign ignorance about planes or submarines. Sometimes it would just be a case of the officer listening to the conversations of the other men, though in this situation it had to obviously be a man who had a good grasp of the German language.

Cover stories were the bane of an interrogator and breaking through them was the first part of exposing a lie. The Germans, particularly the Abwehr, were not masterful with providing their men with covers. They often relied on simplistic and shallow tales, giving the agent a potted knowl-edge of London that would unravel when he was pressed, or claiming he was an Englishman when his accent was so strong as to make this seem laughable to a wartime nation. There is the wonderful tale of the POWs who successfully escaped from their camp and tried to reach Ireland claim-ing to be French. Only one of them spoke a pittance of the language and when accosted by the police and some French natives, rapidly ran out of lies to spin out his story. When he couldn't even describe the region he had supposedly lived in he was promptly arrested.

A more depressing story (at least when it comes to espionage skills) occurred when two German spies were landed in Britain in the early days of the war. One spoke a little English, his comrade none. They had few supplies when they parachuted in and very soon both men were suffering from thirst. The English-speaking spy went to a pub and asked for beer, not realising that it was too early in the morning for him to be served. The pub landlord was not only suspicious of the man's lack of pub knowledge, but of his accent. The spy was told to return later and when he did the police were waiting for him.

His comrade eked it out in country ditches for a little longer, in despair and utterly helpless without a word of English, before he gave himself up.

Breaking a cover story required the interrogator to know more about it than his suspect. If the spy claimed an extensive knowledge of Edinburgh then the interrogator had to spend time scouring maps, guidebooks, photographs and any other material available to him just so he could reach that crucial moment in an interview when he could say – 'you are lying, you have never been there!'

Occasionally, adept spies would prove problematic. The traitor Hansen, when captured, immediately admitted to his interrogator that he had had in his possession a wireless telegraphy (W/T) set, hoping this helpful information, along with his pronouncement that he despised the Germans and had been forced into helping them, would result in his early freedom. At which point he intended to go back to the site where he had hidden the W/T device and retrieve it. It was certainly cunning, but fortunately the interrogators felt it all sounded a little too plausible and kept him under lock and key.

Most methods had their psychological element; misplaced trust, induced outrage or angry disbelief were all emotions the interrogators would play on to get results. The deliberate interrogation of the wrong prisoner was one such example. Two POWs would be placed in the same cell and in the dead of night one would be removed for questioning. This prisoner would be presented to an interrogator who appeared drunk and who badgered him with questions that the POW could not answer, but that his cellmate could – as the interrogators knew all too well. After half an hour of being shouted at and bullied the prisoner would be returned to his cell feeling righteously indignant and his likely reaction would be to tell his cellmate exactly what had just happened.

The cellmate, it was hoped, would realise the prison guards had brought the wrong man to the interrogator and he would be both amused and delighted at having avoided the questions. In many cases he would then tell his unfortunate comrade what the correct answers to the questions were, while a discreet microphone listened in and recorded all.

A more complicated strategy along the same theme involved rigging the printing of fake newspapers. A few copies of a daily paper would have a spoof article printed inside and would be given to specific POWs who were kept in cells rigged with microphones. The idea was the prisoners would reach the fake article and comment on it. Such was the case in late 1941 when a fake article was printed containing an alleged Admiralty communiqué detailing the identification number of U-boats that had been sunk, along with the names of their commanders. While most of the report was genuine a few numbers and names were deliberately wrong. The rigged paper was given to two U-boat officers who laughed when they found the incorrect article and keenly discussed it. The result was that the British were able to obtain an almost complete list of U-boats still operating at the time.

The downside to this method was felt in the latter years of the war when the British were attempting to weaken National Socialist support. They attempted to reduce the number of ardent Nazis in the camps by providing prisoners with newspapers containing accurate updates on the war's progress and the horrors of Hitler's regime. Quite a few prisoners believed these papers were fakes designed for propaganda and, after the interrogators' previous use of such papers to extract information, you can hardly blame them.

The darkest element in the interrogators' catalogue of psychological games was the use of a belief in the supernatural to unnerve a man. At Camp 020 this was 'The Legend of Cell Fourteen'; it is remarkable that a melodramatic fable created by the chance happenstance of the camp building containing an old padded cell should have proved so successful. The unfortunate spy who was initiated into the Cell Fourteen legend was presented with a story straight out of a horror movie.

It began with a simple phrase – 'you will now be sent to Cell Fourteen' – before the story unfolded. First the interrogator explains that Cell Fourteen was used in peacetime for mad men, its walls were padded to stop them from bashing their brains out. Some of the lunatics who resided in that cell duly recovered, some, despite the best efforts of the warders, committed suicide, while others died of unexplained yet completely natural causes. Fortunately, the cell was situated just opposite the mortuary for convenience.

The interrogator then goes on to apologetically say that the wartime situation has forced them to bring old Cell Fourteen back into service. The padding on the walls has gone and the room appears like any other; maybe it seems a little more remote, a little more cold and dark than the others, but really it is no different. Odd though, that people persist in spreading rumours that it has a sinister reputation …

Other spies, he continues, believe there is a supernatural presence in the room; they believe a 'psychic element' is active. Others just find it a claustrophobic space, which is peculiar because it is no different from the other rooms, and then there are those spies who suffer from a guilty conscience and can seem to find no rest in Cell Fourteen. Results from the room are quite interesting: some spies experience a revelation and tell the truth, which enables them to be transferred from the cell, others have unfortunately committed suicide, while others have gone from Cell Fourteen to their final destination with the hangman.

By now, hoping a chill is running down his suspect's back, the interrogator presents the *coup de grâce* by announcing that he will not see the spy again, nor can he say how long he will be kept in Cell Fourteen. Petitions will not be heard. The only exit is through a written confession.

Theatrical indeed! It seems absurd that a ludicrous story about a haunted cell could have ever been considered a productive interrogation tool. Yet it worked; after hearing the story men lost their arrogance, their composure, some even shuddered with fear. It helped that Cell Fourteen's story was circulating among the prisoners anyway, and the power of gossip is never to be underestimated. Cell Fourteen broke many men simply because of a story. It was a final move in the interrogation game and if it failed then the break of a spy was deemed impossible.

The man who devised Cell Fourteen and its 'history' was an interrogator who had spotted the room and asked himself, 'if I were a captured spy, what would I hate most in my predicament?' It turns out a night with the supernatural was the answer. At least it worked better than the other unorthodox method interrogators sometimes used, which was to get a man drunk. Contrary to appearances portrayed by film and television, it invariably failed to produce a result. It seems that if you want a man to talk there is only one type of spirit you should turn to.

Notes
1 Lieutenant Colonel Stephens (ed.), *A Digest of Ham*.
3 Hervie Haufler, *The Spies Who Never Were*, EReads, 2011.
4 Ibid.
5 Ibid.
6 Lieutenant Colonel Stephens (ed.), *A Digest of Ham*.
7 Ibid.

3

THE SMALLEST DETAIL

'You mentioned something about your unit a few minutes ago, oberleut-nant.' Squadron Leader Hawkes calmly stated to his prisoner Franz von Werra, flying ace and Luftwaffe celebrity, now trapped in the London Cage.

Von Werra was furious with frustration. Since his capture he had reso-lutely refused to give anything but the barest of information, yet Hawkes persisted in questioning him on topics he would not speak about.

'I tell you, I can't reveal …' He snapped, but Hawkes was uninterested and carried on as though he had not been interrupted.

'… and that set me wondering which of your friends at headquarters *Staffel* of the Second *Gruppe* of Number Three Fighter *Geschwader* will look after Simba, your lion cub, now that your deathless exploits with that unit have come to an end – "Sanni" perhaps?'[1]

Von Werra was stunned, as Hawkes had intended. Not only was his unit and specific section known to his British interrogator, but the name and species of his unusual pet and the nickname of his best friend. It was a shocking revelation and one that unnerved him, as it would unnerve many who came through the British interrogation system.

Some POWs imagined that the British had a sophisticated spy network operating within the Nazi ranks; others viewed their interrogators' knowl-edge with such awe that they could almost imagine the British intelligence service as semi-psychic. In fact it was not a clever or extensive spy net-work that provided Hawkes with all his information, though the British did operate a number of agents in Germany; rather it was a group of dedicated intelligence officers working away in stuffy offices. With a large number of women making up their numbers, all of whom were proficient in German, they listened to radio broadcasts, German news, intercepted military signals and conversations between already captured prisoners. They scoured German papers and magazines for useful titbits of information (which was how they discovered so much about Franz von Werra as he had been featured on the cover of German radio magazine *hör mit mir*) and also went through every scrap of paper they found in the pockets of POWs when they first arrived. The minutiae of a man's life, from bus tickets to dinner receipts, were carefully collected and analysed for anything useful – the bus ticket could indicate where the man was based by its route, the dinner receipt his financial picture and even his associates. Each scrap came together to form a convoluted jigsaw puzzle that could eventually provide vital intelligence or break a prisoner into talking.

This attention to detail was what the Gestapo lacked, and Hanns Scharff of the Luftwaffe recognised as essential, but it was an arduous job and needed the mind of a detective or crime novelist to jumble together the mismatched clues. Like the Second World War versions of Sherlock Holmes, the intelligence men and women had to see beyond the ordinariness of the details and develop their significance. Only then could they provide the key information the interrogators needed or back up claims revealed under questioning.

Franz von Werra's case is a prime example of this painstaking unravelling of a man's life and, as it is so well recorded by the man himself, provides a clear picture of the work of the interrogation teams.

Von Werra had been startled by Hawkes' revelation and it temporarily threw him. Indeed, so much so that he slipped straight into a trap laid by his interrogator to determine if he really was of Swiss origin. But his chagrin quickly turned to anger and a determination not to say another word. He was also determined to lie and pretend he knew nothing of a lion cub, or 'Sanni', even if his interrogator might have trouble believing that.

Hawkes then presented him with a copy of *hör mit mir*, the cover of which showed a Luftwaffe leutnant nonchalantly leaning against the wing of his Messerschmitt 109 fighter. He was holding a lion cub that snarled into the camera, and the editor had placed the following caption beneath the picture: 'This is the *Staffel* lion, Simba, taking the place of the British Lion, who seldom shows himself in the vicinity of German Fighter Pilots.'[2]

Von Werra decided to play down the significance, dismissing the man in the picture as not even looking like him and pointing out the man only wore the insignia of a leutnant, while von Werra was a proud oberleutnant. Hawkes was unfazed, calmly asking if von Werra would like to explain when he received his promotion or whether he should tell him.

He then produced a second picture, this time clipped from a magazine. The image showed a Luftwaffe pilot with his hand resting on a Messerschmitt 109 wing, but von Werra was unimpressed as the entire upper portion of the man's face was obscured by a the barrel of a cannon. But that was not what interested Hawkes – it was the man's hand. Though the image was small it had been carefully scoured for clues and the fighter pilot's right hand proved particularly significant. The Luftwaffe man wore a massive signet ring on his third finger with a square stone engraved with a crest, the same ring that von Werra was wearing, now uncomfortably, on his hand. But even more damning was the odd position of the man's forefinger, which stuck out awkwardly straight as though the pilot was not able to bend it at the knuckle. Hawkes must have been smiling with triumph; he had offered von Werra a cigarette at the start of the interview and the German had taken it and smoked it, all the time with his forefinger stiffly stuck out. The permanently damaged finger was also recorded in the medical examination he had undergone when he arrived at the London Cage. There was no use denying it, Franz von Werra was the man in the pictures and the British knew far more about him than he would have liked.

They also knew he was a habitual liar and keen on self-aggrandisement. While not so significant from an intelligence point of view, Hawkes now began to set out his case for von Werra, the fantastic storyteller, to further cripple the man's morale and break him.

Hawkes presented his prisoner with a transcript of a German radio broadcast from 30 August, just eight days prior to their conversation. It was a report about a recent German raid over England and von Werra had personally explained the details to radio listeners. He had told a fabulous story about being separated from his formation and flying unexpectedly over a British aerodrome. Attaching himself to a formation of six British fighters who were circling to land, he opened fire and took out the last two planes, which burst into flames; a third plane he hit just as it landed, but it failed to ignite. He then calmly flew to the edge of the aerodrome where he had seen aircraft taxiing. Three planes were parked beside a tent and a mobile petrol tank; von Werra machine-gunned all of them, and petrol from the tanker set fire to the planes. Another low sweep enabled him to take out a sixth plane, but by this point the British were manning machine guns so he took off for home.

Asked by his interviewer how many planes he shot down, he was confident he had shot down three, but it was more likely four, not including those set alight by the burning petrol tanker. It was, of course, a complete and utter lie. Needless to say, Franz von Werra was shocked by the thoroughness of the British and their ruthless attention to detail.

Von Werra was arrogant and full of bombast, a trait that was shared by many of the early prisoners who came through British hands. This trait was accentuated by German propaganda and the widely held belief among the various military ranks and also civilians that the war would be short, with little German bloodshed or enemy resistance. Early victories only heightened this idea and the constant reiterating of British incompetence, stupidity and farcical military power through the popular media only sharpened the misconception. Those first soldiers, sailors and pilots viewed war as a minor interlude in their lives.

The German war machine also played down Britain's intelligence network as part of the berating and belittling of the enemy – this would be a major miscalculation as it generated over-confidence in captured Germans. While British brutality and predilection for torture was repeated time and time again to troops, making capture a dreaded prospect (and perhaps in the minds of some officers, making it more likely their men would die before being captured), the actual skill and sophistication of the British interrogation system was brushed over. The British were ignorant, weak fools and no German need fear them, especially with invasion and victory such a short distance away.

POWs often took this prediction as gospel, and therefore took risks that an otherwise more cautious man would not. In particular they hardly ever bothered to destroy any documents they were carrying upon being captured. Von Werra was an exception to this, but he stood out from the crowd as being less gullible and more cynical of the Nazi war mantras. Even so, his happiness to appear in magazine photo shoots and broadcast fantastical stories of solo air raids was again an underestimation of the British skill at information gathering.

Yet his comrades were even worse. Most arrived with an array of snippets of useful information dispersed about their clothing. All the paraphernalia of life could be found on a German airman – his bus ticket, a cinema ticket stub, a receipt from the last shop he was in, sometimes maps, or even his written orders. It was an intelligence bounty for the British who made full use of the blithe arrogance of their enemy. Many a Luftwaffe location was unravelled from a town name on a cinema stub, or the printed address of a shop on a receipt.

German secret agents were not a great deal better. Yeo-Thomas, the British agent working with the French Resistance mentioned in the previous chapter, made a point when training up Resistance spies to emphasise the need to avoid reliance on written instructions. Records should not be kept at all, not under any circumstance. Pencilled notes or an aide-memoire could be a vital clue to interrogators and could also sentence an agent to torture and death.

A tragic example of this was a scribbled phone number on a 10 franc note in Yeo-Thomas' possession when he was captured by the Gestapo. It was an innocent coincidence (the number had no connection to the Resistance), but unfortunately the Germans refused to believe that, traced the number and dragged in a baffled and completely innocent French musician, who was tortured but could obviously provide no useful information. Though it is not known what became of him, he was probably murdered to cover up the Gestapo's mistake.

When a suspected German spy was brought to Camp 020 the first procedure was to do a full search, not only for useful documents but for incriminating clues. Property was removed, sorted and listed; a full body search was then conducted. One spy, Nikolai Hansen, had secret ink concealed in the cavity of a tooth – a clear giveaway of his espionage intentions. Another agent had cotton impregnated with secret ink threaded into his collar. The smallest detail could be a clue, and yet spies could also try and get away with the oldest of tricks. The agent Gilinsky slipped past security in Trinidad and even customs in England with $40,000 hidden beneath a false bottom in his trunk, while other agents persisted in hiding papers in their underwear (usually without success), but agent Pigrau Blay was particularly cunning as he had a password hidden in the fly-buttons of his trousers.

The interrogators were obsessive in their art; in his *A Digest of Ham* Lieutenant Colonel Stephens emphasised the need to study every odd note, doodle or random drawing for significance: 'A trivial entry in one page of a notebook coupled with another in a distant page may well be the key to a code; and if it is discovered, it is at once a trump card for a break [of a suspect].'[3]

A prime example of this meticulous study was that of Osmar Hellmuth. Hellmuth had been a rather obscure insurance agent until he was abruptly promoted to diplomatic status (ruffling a few feathers in the process) by the German secret service and sent to Argentina. His surprise promotion and the observation that the German Embassy in Argentina disapproved of him and his mission caused an already suspicious MI5 to persuade the Foreign Office to let them arrest Hellmuth. For a long time the South America Nazi spy ring and its connections with various officials, including ministers in the Argentine Cabinet, had worried Britain. Now they had a prime source of exclusive information, if only they could break him.

Hellmuth was understandably reluctant to admit much, but he did reveal a nugget of information that had been desired for a long time – the name of the chief of the SD in Argentina. Hellmuth explained that he had been due in Spain and upon arrival he was to be greeted by a man with the coded message: '*Saludos de parte del Senor Siegmund Becker*' (Greetings from Herr Siegmund Becker). He was to reply: '*Ah, si, el Hauptsturmführer*' (Ah, yes, the Hauptsturmführer).

The interrogators were intrigued, but no piece of intelligence could be trusted unless confirmed by a reliable source. Hellmuth's word alone was not enough, especially with such a vital piece of information and when a mistake or deliberate deception could be seriously detrimental.

The interrogators returned to Hellmuth's possessions to obtain some form of corroboration; among them was a cardboard folder with five words scribbled on it in pencil. At first glance they seemed irrelevant; the Spanish words were '*Seguismundo*', '*Panadero*', '*Principal*', '*Temporal*' and '*Conductor*'. But the case officers at Camp 020 knew the importance of leaving no stone unturned and one had the idea of translating the words into English and German. They came out as:

Spanish	English	German
Seguismundo	Sigismond	Siegmund
Panadero	Baker	Becker
Principal	Chief	Haupt
Temporal	Storm	Sturm
Conductor	Leader	Führer

Hellmuth had attempted to hide his German code word by translating it into Spanish. When confronted, Hellmuth admitted he had committed the cardinal spying sin – he had written down his password. Though of German birth, Hellmuth's knowledge of his native language was limited (he lived in South America) and he was fearful that his memory would let him down, so he had written out his secret message.

Yet further corroboration came from the investigation of another man's papers. Diego Beltran Leiro was known as an SD courier and in his possession were dozens of photographs, two of which Hellmuth identified as portraying his employer, Becker.

The whole conspiracy came crashing down around the German and Argentine officials. Details were released to the press, questions were asked in Parliament, and the Argentine president had no choice but to summarily dismiss and disown Hellmuth. But it was too late; Cabinet ministers had to resign and a crumbling Argentine government was forced to do what it should have done a long time before – sever diplomatic relations with the Third Reich. Soon the whole government was quietly removed and replaced.

Meanwhile, in Germany the blow was sorely felt. With their South American connection severed, their espionage plans suddenly seemed incredibly fragile. Ribbentrop, Foreign Minister of Germany, blamed the Abwehr; the Abwehr were in turn infuriated as they had been cut out of the Hellmuth business by the SD. Himmler himself became involved, fanning the flames of recrimination which resulted in the Abwehr chief, Admiral Canaris, being dismissed under a cloud of accusations of failure. The triumph for the British was immense and it was largely due to five words scribbled on a cardboard folder.

In many respects, however, that was a minor triumph when compared to the detailed unravelling of another suspect's case. Hellmuth, after all, had already partially admitted the truth, but when a man refused to speak and his connection with the German secret service could not be decisively obtained, the interrogators had to go to work on every detail they could find and hope for proof, or else release a spy for lack of evidence.

This was the case of Manoel Mesquita Dos Santos (usually referred to as just Mesquita), a Portuguese journalist living in Brazil. His financial difficulties made him an easy victim of the Nazi espionage system, who recruited him with promises of attractive payments. Usually when interrogators were faced with such mercenary spies, bought with money rather than national loyalty, they were easy to break. Once it became obvious their benefactors would no longer be interested in them, they would spill their tale and hope to be given the option of working as a double agent.

Such was not the case with Mesquita. He was an intelligent man and a talented journalist, whose loyalty to the Nazi cause was minimal. He had been trained in secret writing and other espionage skills at Rio de Janeiro and then sent to South Africa with the high hopes of German intelligence resting upon him. He was supposed to infiltrate the Union of South Africa (now the Republic of South Africa), which was a British dominion, yet on arriving at Lourenco Marques (now Maputo), the capital city of Mozambique, he discovered that entry into the Union was not as easy as he or the Germans had anticipated. Travel details were never a strong point of the German espionage system.

Mesquita rapidly lost interest in espionage, though felt no harm in tapping his German handlers for £200, which he used to tour the Portuguese colony for his own personal interests, before finally attempting to return to Portugal. He was intercepted by MI5, who deposited him at Camp 020. Yet despite his clear lack of enthusiasm for spying for the Germans, he refused to talk on the subject or admit he had any connection to them. He was aware that the evidence against him was flimsy and by keeping quiet he probably hoped to escape the interrogators and return to Portugal, perhaps to continue draining German intelligence funds for his own purposes.

The British were stumped and particularly anxious as Mesquita had arrived at a time when the Foreign Office was having problems with Portuguese nationals accused of spying. They ideally needed a written confession from Mesquita to enable them to round up more Portuguese spies without causing a diplomatic furore.

There was one option they had left to explore: it had been noted that Mesquita had travelled to Lourenco Marques in the same ship as another spy they had in their custody, Sobhy Hanna. Everything that had been found with Hanna on arrival at Camp 020 was now re-examined in the hope of discovering a clue that would prove Mesquita was a spy.

Among the belongings was a certificate that had been issued to all passengers as a souvenir of 'crossing the line' – part of an onboard ceremony for crossing the equator. The custom of the time was to sit at an equatorial dinner and pass a certificate around to be signed by other passengers. When the interrogators saw this they knew there was a slight chance that Mesquita may have absent-mindedly signed the certificate. After all, what seemed more harmless than scrawling a name on a slip of paper?

The odds were still remote, but with desperation fuelling their optimism the case officers compared the signature in Mesquita's passport to the ones on the certificate. They were lucky: Mesquita had indeed signed the document, but that alone would not break him. He could still argue his innocence; after all there were many innocent names on Hanna's crossing the line certificate.

A degree of deception was in order. Mesquita was told that he had been tailed by a British agent for a considerable time and that this agent had managed to work himself so successfully into Mesquita's life that he had even obtained his signature, the certificate being used to verify the lie. Another dose of good fortune helped to strengthen the case. An agent going by the code name 'Tome' had sent a telegram to Lisbon. When cross referenced against intercepted German communications, the case officers were able to confirm that 'Tome' was Mesquita's rather unimaginative spy name.

Mesquita was presented with his secret identity when interrogated by Camp 020's commandant and then asked to sign his name on a piece of paper. As expected, he deliberately produced a false signature, so his passport and the certificate were presented before him. Completely off-balance by these two most damning slips of evidence and further thrown by the story of being pursued by a British agent, Mesquita lost his composure and wrote out a full confession.

The Foreign Office could now present this confession to the Portuguese ambassador, who would no longer be able to quibble about any of his people being arrested and investigated. Mesquita's case could also now be explored in further depth and expose the level of Portuguese assistance being given to the Nazis.

The Significance of Oliver Strachey

As has already been mentioned, a great deal of the details that exposed spies or broke a POW into revealing war secrets came from intercepted German communications. A great deal of attention has been paid in other works to the breakthrough of the Enigma machine, which resulted in significant intelligence on the German war machine being obtained and used. But while the success of cracking the Enigma codes is indeed a hugely important aspect of wartime cryptography, it was by no means the only aspect.

In fact what is usually considered the first British decryption of a German communiqué happened in the spring of 1940. When a decrypted Abwehr message was issued on 14 April, it opened a whole new world for the interrogators, revealing to them vital information that otherwise would have remained hidden. It also enabled them to hack back into the German communication system to instigate their Double-Cross plan, using turned German agents to feed back false information. Without those messages the interrogators would have been at a major disadvantage.

Yet the decrypting of the early codes, like so much of the war intelligence effort, relied on luck and fortuitous coincidence. It was the role of Section C of the Signals Intelligence Service (MI8) to collect German messages by recording enemy wireless transmissions. Many messages were encoded and MI8-C Section was merely a recording department, which relied on other divisions to break the codes. Undecipherable messages were set to one side for someone else to deal with and, alarmingly, were often overlooked just because they were encoded, despite it being clear they must hold some importance.

One 25-year-old, Hugh Redwald Trevor-Roper, worked in MI8-C as a lowly junior member of staff. He became intrigued by a large number of mumbo-jumbo texts that were being ignored simply because they were so unreadable. He had no knowledge of cryptography and his own attempts to crack the messages failed miserably; his only insight was that they appeared to not follow the pattern of standard military signals, diplomatic messages or even commercial telegrams. Trevor-Roper realised the messages would be best off in the hands of an experienced cryptographer, but he was too junior a member of MI8 to authorise the odd intercepts being removed from C Section, despite them being continually overlooked as the department worked busily to collect messages they could read.

Once again good fortune played a role, as Trevor-Roper's supervisor happened to be Major Gill, an enterprising and unconventional officer, who was prepared to listen to young Hugh's thoughts on the encrypted messages. He agreed to send samples of the intercepts to Commander Alastair Denniston at the Government Code and Cypher School. The school was situated in Berkeley Street and was headquarters for the finest codebreakers in Britain.

At the school the odd intercepts ended up on the desk of Oliver Strachey, a man whose name would later become synonymous with decrypts and who the interrogators referred to fondly when using German intelligence intercepts to break prisoners.

Oliver Strachey (1874–1960), son of Lieutenant General Sir Richard Strachey and Lady Jane Strachey, was brother to the writer and critic Lytton Strachey and began his cryptography career with the British military intelligence service during the First World War. During the war he worked at the Government Code and Cypher School, where he would still be when the Second World War broke out. He was the star of the code breaking world and along with Dillwyn 'Dilly' Knox formed a remarkable and, some say, incomparable cryptanalyst partnership. Yet with Trevor-Roper's 'oddities' he slipped up.

The messages wound up in Strachey's in-tray, ignored and forgotten, just like they had been at C Section. Only when politely nudged did he examine them and conclude they must be Russian signals sent from Shanghai. He went on to write to Major Gill: 'It is not thought that they are German.'[4]

It took some courage to consider that the celebrated code cracker could be wrong, but Major Gill had been convinced by Trevor-Roper that there was something important in these cast-aside notes. During the First World War he had had some experience of cryptanalysis and with the enthusiasm of an amateur he decided to prove the eminent Strachey wrong. His decision was probably helped by the fact that he shared a flat with Trevor-Roper and the young man's ceaseless curiosity about the intercepts rubbed off. Against protocol he took the 'Russian' messages home and with Hugh spent all his free evenings endeavouring to decode them.

Their first successes came at Christmas 1939 when they made headway breaking into the cipher and they solved it fully in early 1940. Reading the decrypted messages, Trevor-Roper was stunned to realise they were dealing with top secret communications between the Abwehr and its stations abroad, as well as most of its agents. The significance was immense; there was nothing 'Russian' about them and that Strachey had failed to recognise the importance of the codes only added to Gill and Trevor-Roper's feelings of triumph.

The cracking of the messages was a step towards the complete compromise of the Abwehr's communications. But it would prove to be only a part of the puzzle. The Abwehr were industrious enough to use three methods of encryption for transmissions – the most famous was the use of a modified Enigma machine to send messages to countries they knew were under strict German control. In rare cases they used specially constructed codebooks called *Satzbuecher*, but by far their most common method for communicating with agents in the field was by a method called paper-and-pencil ciphers. An agent was issued with a specific popular book that was readily available (a Bible or classic novels were usual). Their coded messages would use the book as their key. It seemed a practical solution to the Abwehr handlers; bulky Enigma machines could not be carried about by agents without drawing attention or falling into the wrong hands, but a book seemed innocuous enough and readily overlooked. In fact the paper-and-pencil method was relatively secure and had Trevor-Roper not been inspired by those gibberish scribblings at C Section the Abwehr could have happily carried on sending secret communications.

It was a critical starting point and when an Enigma machine was captured in 1941 from a U-boat it enabled British intelligence to fill another gap in their knowledge. By early 1942, code-breaker Dilly Knox could confidently say that all Abwehr codes and ciphers had been compromised and the internal workings of German intelligence were at their mercy. Now they were able to not only listen and understand secret wireless messages, but they could learn of paper-based communications, which they could intercept via the wartime censoring system or, in desperation, by speedy tampering and returning of suspect documents. Messages coded with secret ink, microphotography or microdotting all began to reveal their hidden words, while the Germans remained supremely confident that their codes were unbreakable.

Meanwhile, Oliver Strachey had been put in charge of a new section at Bletchley Park where intercepted messages were routinely decoded and passed on to the relevant departments. This became ISOS, or Intelligence (sometimes Illicit) Services Oliver Strachey. Throughout the war ISOS was the code name interrogators used for referring to information Bletchley Park had sent to them. ISOS decrypted messages from the Abwehr, SD and RSHA. There was also ISK, Intelligence Service Knox, named after Dilly in recognition of his work to crack the Enigma code. The ISK issued Enigma decrypts.

Very rapidly ISOS became an essential tool in the interrogators' kit. It could be used to spark information or to check it, and a number of enemy agents fell into the hands of the British through the efforts of ISOS. One example was Axel Coll, who, along with a number of German wireless operators involved in meteorological studies, was captured by a Norwegian gunboat while he was travelling on the SS *Vesle Kari* near Greenland. Coll arrived in England with two other wireless operators. British-intercepted German transmissions confirmed that he should really be at Camp 020 facing an espionage charge. Coll was open to interrogation and soon revealed valuable information on the *Vesle Kari's* Arctic voyage. He also confirmed the interrogators' dim views of German spies by telling them an elaborate story about how he was really supposed to captain a ship servicing the meteorological stations in Greenland, but instead he had been given a camera, even though he was no photographer, and told to take pictures of the voyage.

A more significant ISOS success was the exposure of Gastao Crawford de Freitas Ferraz, whose espionage activities could have easily jeopardised the Allied landing in North Africa. De Freitas was a radio operator on the SS *Gil Eannes*, a depot ship of the Portuguese Cod Fishing Fleet (and yet another reason why the Foreign Office was anxious about the loyalty of Portuguese nationals). The vessel was the perfect cover for de Freitas' undercover activities; the fleet had strong diplomatic backing through a reciprocal agreement with the British fishing fleet off Azores and a personal guarantee through two Portuguese naval officers that 'no vessel of the fleet which they administered would be guilty of unneutral conduct'.[5]

With such strong support and the possibility of a diplomatic furore should a seemingly innocent man from a 'neutral' country be arrested, the interrogators knew they would need solid evidence before they dared lay a finger on de Freitas. ISOS had been monitoring the situation and knew that one of the radio operators on the *Gil Eannes* (there were two) was guilty of corresponding with the Germans. Yet all they had was a cover name that they felt reasonably confident could be linked with de Freitas. It was not much to go on, but ISOS had a reputation for extreme reliability; the teams at Bletchley rarely got things wrong and the situation was too risky to overlook.

De Freitas was arrested by the Royal Navy just hours before the *Gil Eannes* would have come into contact with the huge convoy of Allied transport ships carrying an invasion force of troops to French North Africa in November 1942.

When de Freitas arrived at Camp 020 the interrogators knew there was a lot resting on their skills; if ISOS was wrong then the backlash could permanently tarnish the trust placed in the signals they translated. De Freitas had made their job harder by jettisoning his code when his ship was stopped and there was nothing of use among his possessions. But there was a single nugget of useful information at their disposal – it was known that one of de Freitas' contacts was Kuno Weltzein and at the start of his first interrogation he was handed a photograph of him and asked if he knew him. De Freitas let out a hysterical wail and descended into anguished sobbing – a tactic others had used to buy themselves time. Seeing that the interview could not progress until de Freitas had composed himself, the prisoner was sent back to his cell. By the next afternoon the interrogators were determined to break him and, using the 'blow hot, blow cold' method Lieutenant Colonel Stephens favoured, de Freitas was cajoled into admitting to spying for the Germans and that he had transmitted two messages to his employers. A written confession was next on the agenda and the broken de Freitas mutely complied. The Foreign Office could breathe a sigh of relief that they wouldn't have to face a diplomatic crisis and the interrogators could smile proudly at the infallibility of ISOS.

To many, ISOS now seemed the ultimate fountain of knowledge when it came to spies, but even the irreproachable ISOS could not conjure confessions from determined captives. One example was Lambertus Elferink (see Chapter 6). ISOS was adamant that he was a spy code-named 'Hamlet', but without a confession from the man himself their information was useless.

Intercepted messages could also be open to misinterpretation. When Josef and Mathilde Gobin found themselves at Camp 020 it was so they could be confronted in their lies and excuses by unimpeachable ISOS information. The Belgian Josef Gobin (described by Stephens as 'rat-like') had first attracted Nazi attention in 1940 and had been trained in radio operation in 1941. He claimed, however, that he was inactive until the Allied occupation of Antwerp in September 1944. This was the first lie ISOS could blow to pieces – they had evidence of earlier operational information being broadcast by Gobin to his German handlers, as well as more messages that he sent between September and October 1944. Apparently his efforts impressed the German secret service enough that they increased his salary from 7,000 francs to 15,000 francs per month – hardly the salary of an inactive agent.

Arriving with his wife at Camp 020, Gobin proved reticent and awkward. Direct confrontation with his German paymaster in Brussels when he was first captured had failed to shake him so the interrogators knew they were in for a challenge. They endeavoured to divide and conquer the couple without success, and then maintained pressure on Gobin to talk at all times. When not in the interrogation room he was confronted by a string of 'well-wishing' fellow inmates who tried to persuade him to talk.

The constant harassment finally broke his morale and Gobin reluctantly dictated a confession, but there was one issue that still bothered the interrogators. ISOS had come across two important agents that Gobin had repeatedly mentioned by code names in communications – 'Sophie' and 'Bertha'. The interrogators' brief mentioned the importance of identifying these agents.

Using the same tactic as that inflicted on Franz von Werra, Gobin's interrogator took the limited information he had and presented it as though he knew everything.

'One of your German contacts has betrayed to us your connection with the agents "Sophie" and "Bertha" and you better explain them in your confession.'[6]

This raised an unfortunate smirk on Gobin's face. Aside from his espionage work he had been a German black market contact; to keep the dealings discreet Gobin had been told to give black market goods code names like agents: 'Sophie' was butter, 'Bertha' was bacon. It was a minor slip by ISOS, but if Gobin had not already been writing his confession, such a mistake could have derailed an interrogation. When presenting themselves as confident, all-knowing personalities the interrogators could not allow the façade to be punctured by a wrong assumption that could undermine everything and resolve the prisoner into not talking.

This was just one of the risks of relying on ISOS intercepts; another was revealing too much and enabling captives to learn about the system. ISOS was a closely guarded secret; no one wanted the Germans to get wind of it as it was a key component of the Double-Cross System. Many agents and many strategic plans could be destroyed if a prisoner learnt of the system and decided to deliver news of it back to the Germans.

The worst happened in early 1944 when the irreproachable and consistently reliable intercepts came into serious question for the first time, however. The culprit was Barone Filippo Manfredi de Blasis. Manfredi was first interviewed by a British intelligence officer in Italy, who had strong ISOS evidence against him. When this failed to extract a confession the intelligence officer was so bemused that he came to the assumption that the barone must be innocent. Even worse, he began championing the Italian nobleman's cause, backed by his intelligence organisation in Italy.

Suddenly ISOS, which had provided so much information against the good barone, was under suspicion of error. Fifty other spy cases, which were largely supported by ISOS information, also came into doubt and MI6 rushed Manfredi to England, not to necessarily prove his crime but to exonerate the ISOS. Panic was obvious; ISOS was heavily relied upon and if it could not be trusted the whole interrogation system and possibly the Double-Cross System could falter and fail. How many agents might slip through the net and cause serious damage to the war effort if that was the case?

ISOS claimed that Manfredi had been approached by the German secret service on 29 August 1943. They wanted him to work behind the 8th Army lines at Cerignola, southern Italy, but British intelligence in Italy painted a different picture, quite damning to ISOS. In one letter the organisation in Italy stated:

> In summing up Manfredi's character the interrogator says that in his opinion it was psychologically impossible for the man to have been a German agent; that he was neither fascist nor pro-German; that he was an impulsive and confiding child, for example, his servants held the keys to his safe; he was temperamentally incapable of keeping any important secret.[7]

MI6 stated its own quandary in another letter:

> Manfredi is the first alleged agent of the SD in Italy to fall into our hands; we regard him as providing us with a test case of the reality or the reverse of the SD's post-operational network ... we have not far short of fifty names of non-Germans in Italy alleged to be involved in the SD. As we advance up Italy we may reasonably expect the question 'how far we can rely on evidence from the ISOS unsupported from any outside source' will become increasingly urgent. If only the question of Manfredi's guilt or innocence can be finally settled, it will be of great assistance to us in dealing with similar cases.[8]

It was a mammoth task the interrogators were faced with when Manfredi came before them: they had to prove ISOS's worth unequivocally or accept that their crack code-breakers could be wrong. At his first interrogation in January 1944 Manfredi was indignant and troublesome. The intelligence agent in Italy had not only believed his innocence but told him as much and now he puffed and pouted and indulged in outraged tantrums.

Determined to elicit the truth one way or another, a co-belligerent within the camp, Capitano Bonzo, was brought in both during interrogations and while Manfredi was in his cell to whittle away his resolve. This proved partly successful when, thirteen days after his arrival, Manfredi handed in a statement talking about his involvement with a man named Koehler. The case officers were not sure of the significance, but after careful debate decided that the commandant would inform Manfredi that he knew Koehler was an agent of the German secret service and therefore Manfredi had, by default, admitted his own contact with the organisation.

The commandant put up a pretence of sympathy – Manfredi, he suggested to the prisoner, was perhaps not deliberately spying for the Germans, but by his coincidental connection could provide useful information. Manfredi blustered out denials, but when Bonzo was brought into the interrogation and joined in trying to persuade him he became confused by this new attack from his own countryman. Eventually the men were dismissed to the same cell where continued pressure (the standard practice at Camp 020), either by Bonzo arguing with Manfredi to tell the truth or further interrogations, was kept up.

Manfredi, harassed on all sides, finally cracked and produced another statement on 23 January. In this he admitted that when Koehler had asked him if he would do anything for his country, Manfredi had unthinkingly answered 'yes'. Koehler then said he would send someone to him in Puglia who would commit acts of sabotage that they were to arrange later. The barone was to employ this man as a watchman, or similar, on his estate to avoid any arousal of suspicion.

Manfredi persisted in playing the role of innocent dupe to his British captors and said he had 'accepted the general idea in order to gain time'. Koehler apparently impressed on him the need to keep this all a secret even from the Italian General Staff, but Manfredi was so spooked that the very next day he informed Colonel de Carlo, who calmly told him 'to let the matter drop'. It seems the Italians were of the same opinion as the British – that Manfredi was slightly simple, prone to manipulation and gullibility, only the Germans, it seemed, took him seriously.

But from ISOS's point of view the case for their defence was proven. They had been accurate in their statements that Manfredi was involved, albeit rather uncomfortably, with the German secret service. There was yet one more blunder to occur, however, in Camp 020, this time of no fault of the ISOS. The original Manfredi case officer had gone off sick and a new interrogator was improperly briefed and began accusing the barone of being the saboteur himself, intent on blowing up bridges on his estate. Manfredi was pushed into a horrendous, hysterical denial in which he almost sobbed, 'In my estate there is no water, there is no need of bridges. Where there are no bridges, they cannot be blown up.'

One other important piece of information came from the mental racking of Manfredi – it seemed his estranged wife was also a paid German spy. She spent a large proportion of her time travelling Europe calling on specialists about her health problems, and on one of these supposed medicinal visits she arrived at Berchtesgaden (a favourite haunt of Hitler's) for a spell of rest and recuperation. Dining out one evening she collapsed and Heinrich Himmler himself came to her aid and put his car at her disposal.

Thrown by this revelation, Manfredi tried to brush it aside as yet another innocent coincidence (he was a great sufferer of them it seemed). Surely, he put it to his interrogators, as it was known Himmler was such a chivalrous gentleman, the loaning of his own car should be viewed as nothing more than a generous gesture? The barone may have even been sincere in this statement; he was certainly gullible enough to believe such a lie. His interrogators, however, were not, and within a short span of time confirmation of their suspicions was obtained.

Manfredi came to be seen as a pathetic figure at Camp 020; even Bonzo, who was sent to become his indispensable companion (and who helped the barone in a bread raid on the prison pantry), confessed that he found the man's company 'more nauseating in the ultimate than it was amusing'. His minimal value as a spy to the Germans, and possibly his genuine ignorance of what he was getting involved with, was not taken into account when he was eventually sent to face whatever justice the Italian General Staff decided to dole out. Ironically, his former cellmate Bonzo was now part of that Staff.

Manfredi may not have been the greatest spy, but his case, like the others briefly mentioned here, proved the importance of scrutinising the minutiae of a man's life. It also showed the trust placed in ISOS, a trust that could be shattered by the misguided beliefs of one British intelligence officer. The world of intelligence was also a world of lies, and sometimes it was hard to put aside cynicism, even when an invaluable source was at stake.

Notes
1 Kendal Burt & James Leasor, *The One that Got Away*, Collins, 1956.
2 Ibid.
3 Lieutenant Colonel Stephens (ed.), *A Digest of Ham*.
4 Ladislas Farago, *The Game of the Foxes*, Hodder & Stoughton, 1971.
5 Lieutenant Colonel Stephens (ed.), *A Digest of Ham*.
6 Ibid.
7 Ibid.
8 Ibid.

4

THE USEFULNESS OF TRAITORS

'My aim was to help shorten the war for my unfortunate countrymen and to help concentration camp inmates avoid further suffering.'[1]

Such was the sentiment of Fritz Kolbe, one of the most influential traitors of the Second World War, a sentiment that many would confess to when captured by the British. Kolbe was an exception to the normal traitor, however, not only because he was in a prime position as a diplomat in the German Foreign Ministry to have access to important documents, but because he was a blatant anti-Nazi who refused to join the Nazi Party and was not afraid to speak of his dislike of the regime. Despite this he was tolerated as a good worker, even if his politics meant he was confined to stamping passports and visas. An anti-Nazi leaflet dropper who railed against Hitler's regime in the back rooms of Berlin pubs, he felt incredibly impotent when faced with the continual horrors and outrages of his contemporaries. He also knew that across his desk passed hundreds of documents that could be of incredible significance to the Allied war effort if only they could see them.

Yet he was in no position to act as a spy; his mundane role in the Foreign Ministry even meant making first contact with the Allies was near enough impossible. He would have remained impotently raging against the regime he served at his desk had a superior Foreign Office employee and fellow Nazi-critic not intervened and put Kolbe's name on the list of privileged officials who could act as diplomatic couriers for the Third Reich.

Kolbe wasted no time in using the opportunity and on the morning of 15 August 1943 he locked his office door and removed his trousers, so he could conceal two envelopes containing mimeographed secret documents by strapping them to his legs. Calmly redressing, he picked up a diplomatic bag containing official dispatches and made his way to Berlin's Anhalter railway station. There he boarded a train decked with swastikas and Nazi flags, symbols of the regime he was about to betray at great risk to himself, and settled into a seat for his official journey to Berne, Switzerland.

No doubt scared, but also triumphantly elated for at last doing something to end the war and the regime he despised, a thousand thoughts must have rushed through Kolbe's mind on that journey, not least the nagging fear of being searched and discovered. However, it is unlikely that he anticipated the reception he would receive at the British Embassy, where he was laughed at and dismissed.

Kolbe must have felt supremely disappointed; he had literally risked his life to bring the documents to the Allies only to be disbelieved. It was not a surprising turn of events for the British were suspicious of walk-ins as the Gestapo had tried to plant agents in Britain in this way. Kolbe also did not go in person, but sent another German, Kocherthaler, on his behalf. Kocherthaler's vague talk about an unspecified friend who could help the Allies no doubt sounded exactly like an agent's cover story and he was dismissed with a polite 'no, thank you'.

Kocherthaler would then try the Americans (who had been warned by the British about a man claiming to have secret information), but this time he contacted a Swiss banker by the name of Dreyfus who worked for the Americans and could provide an introduction. Even with Dreyfus calling the Americans and informing them of his 'friend' who could be useful to them, Kocherthaler was treated with suspicion. It wasn't until he laid out three sample documents Kolbe had loaned him as evidence of the value of the information his friend could obtain that the Americans grew excited and, after hasty deliberations, welcomed Kolbe into their fold of spies.

Kolbe's complicated story, with so many about-turns and near-misses, was typical of the attitude shown to traitors who claimed they wanted to help the Allies.

Lieutenant Colonel Stephens wrote about the use of traitors as stool pigeons: 'Essentially [the traitor] is a despicable character, treacherous to a degree, mistrusted by both sides, and a lasting anxiety to any adminis-tration.'[2] Walks-in, turncoats, captured soldiers, those who protested their ardent anti-Nazi feelings; the British met them all and over the course of the war became rather immune to their stories of detesting Hitler, desiring peace, and their vainly noble talk of wanting to save the world by passing on information. Yet, each traitor had to be taken with at least a pinch of seri-ousness, or else something vital could be missed and, ultimately, a reliable traitor could be vital to derailing the Nazi war effort.

A Captive Audience

One of Hitler's greatest weaknesses was his belief in the power of fear. Loyalty through fear was a key factor in the recruiting of spies and the maintaining of discipline among soldiers. Death threats aimed at the person themselves or at their family could produce a facsimile of loyalty, at least while the person was within reach of the Nazi machine, but once beyond its scope that façade of loyalty would quickly diminish and falter.

One example of this 'loyalty by fear' was given by Lieutenant Corporal Walter Modler of 11 Coy, 891 Gren. Regiment, who explained: 'On 15 Feb '44, 11 Coy made a formal complaint to the effect that they had been issued with NO [sic] cigarettes or spirit ration for the month, although the officers appeared to have plentiful supplies. The Coy Comd's reply was to have the whole Coy paraded, and threaten to have every tenth man shot if there were any repetition of the complaint. Generally speaking, severe punishments were awarded for the most trifling offences. One man received 14 days in a detention camp for having put some personal belongings into his respirator bag.'[3]

Modler was 36 years old and, when captured, expressed strong anti-Nazi feelings; the interrogators felt his statements reliable.

Morale was indeed becoming difficult to maintain within the German army as the war progressed. The war that would be 'finished in a fortnight' was dragging on and on, and many of the men were not even sure what they were fighting for. Hitler was topping up his armed forces with con-scripts from invaded countries; men who were bullied into military service and who endeavoured to be captured as soon as possible. Among them were captured Russians who were given the choice of starving to death in a prison camp or joining the Nazi army – it was hardly a difficult decision.

The more disgruntled the soldiers became, the more their officers (many of whom had only limited military experience and had been promoted because they knew the right people) relied on violent threats and severe punishments to keep the men in line. The cumulative result was an army that looked to be captured and that upon imprisonment readily gave up their information, often seeming to enjoy complaining about their officers.

Yet again Germany played into the British interrogators' hands, this time by making their men open and willing to talking with the enemy. Of course, any man who gave up information readily was, technically, a traitor, though they themselves may not have recognised the fact. Others were deliberate deserters who had risked death to speak with the British.

One such example was an unnamed POW who had arranged to desert. (The fact he was unnamed in the files suggests the British may have had plans for him; most interrogated POWs were named, unless the report was dealing with a large group and collating the information given.)

Interrogated on 29 April 1943, the deserter revealed he had volunteered for the German air force upon the outbreak of war and was trained in signals, wireless telegraphy and radio telegraphy. There was a marked difference in the way he spoke about his early days in the air force and about his later time. On the one hand he was happy to reveal information about the base he worked in, the number of men and women, their duties (largely listening to R/T messages from British planes) and the effectiveness of deliberately produced British interference, which reduced the listeners' ability to hear transmissions by 30%. Yet when asked about his time training and the locations of his schools he showed marked reticence, even though this information could be regarded as being far less vital.

It seems that even in the mind of a deserter there was a certain kind of loyalty for the early war effort that faded as the years passed. Part of the problem for the German military was a general apathy and depression that had sunk in on the men. In another interrogation report, dated 30 March 1944, which combined the testimony of twenty-two prisoners of war to create a lucid intelligence narrative, it was noted: 'The military developments of the last few months have convinced most of these men that a German victory is no longer possible.'[4]

This all fed into the popular view that there was very little point in with-holding information from the British interrogators; indeed, some considered providing what little they knew about the Nazi war machine a viable way to end the war sooner rather than later and enable them to go home.

In a 1944 report discussing the growing problem the Germans were facing from guerrilla partisan attacks in north Croatia and Slavonia it was pointed out: 'Fear of the partisans among German soldiers, and especially their officers, is tremendous. The chances of surrendering to British troops are discussed almost openly.'[5]

The men from this particular unit were largely Austrian and they had other issues that made them easy prey for a sympathetic British ear: 'PWs from the Austrian provinces spoke with deep hatred of the things that had been done to them. PW stated there was a shortage of everything in his home district, but NO signs of starvation. Bread especially was so bad as to be also uneatable. Food rationing, it was thought, was being carried out with exceptional severity in Austrian villages. PW said that feeling among the peasantry against their German masters was so strong that, given the opportunity, even the old men would be glad to take up arms against them.'

Bitterness and a sense of being unfairly treated opened the men's mouths; the only reticence came when a prisoner feared he would suffer a reprisal for some action he had taken during the conflict. Whether this was carrying out orders to massacre villagers or using brutality against captives, in these instances a sense of self-preservation rather than loyalty would stopper a man's voice. When, after the war, the interrogators turned their attentions away from military secrets to war crimes, they would find this a common theme with their new prisoners. Though in that instance reticence could not spare a man the noose.

Deliberate traitors, those who arranged to be captured and even kept useful information in the hope it would aid the Allies, came in all shapes and sizes. They were not particularly uncommon and arrived in British hands for a variety of reasons.

Perhaps the most famous voluntary captive (though he did not consider becoming one when he started out) was Rudolf Hess, Hitler's deluded deputy, who flew to Scotland in 1941 believing he could broker a peace deal between Britain and Germany. A rather tragic figure in the Nazi regime, he probably didn't deserve to be lumped with the other monstrous war criminals who found themselves answering for their actions in Nuremberg. Hess strikes a modern reader as always having a somewhat dubious mental stability; his flight to Scotland on the mistaken belief that a powerful peace party existed in Britain and wanted to negotiate with Germany is just one example. He comes across as naïve and utterly devoted to Hitler, though not so to his National Socialist ideals. He was not an exact traitor, though his arrival and capture aroused a great deal of commotion, and interrogators were optimistic of what valuable information he could be coerced into giving.

As it was, Hess proved to be a lightweight figure in Nazi politics, kept about because of his friendship with Hitler, and most of his contemporaries felt that his influence on any major state decisions was slight to say the least. Hess would eventually retreat into amnesia to avoid his interrogators' questions and even denied knowing Goering when he was confronted with him.

A German who truly wanted to be captured was Uffz Franke, a cipherer who ended up in a panzer division in Africa. Despite having been in the military since 1937, Franke was adamantly anti-Nazi and spent most of 1941 in prison for 'expressing views prejudicial to the regime'. This was a recurring theme, with many eventual deserters pointing out their jail sentence or time in a detention camp as evidence of their anti-Nazi feelings. It also sums up the desperation for troops as the years ticked by, that so many of these outspoken men were absorbed back into the ranks despite their evident danger for causing dissention or betrayal.

This was exactly the case with Franke. He served a year in prison, was released in March 1942 and in May of that year was sent to Africa. By December he had 'arranged' his capture by the British, though the specifics of this are not mentioned in the file; a possible scenario was that Franke learned of the location of British troops and fled his unit to surrender to them. In such circumstances he was effectively equivalent to a 'walk-in' at an embassy and was treated with necessary suspicion.

How ever he ended up there, Franke was eventually sent to Cairo for interrogation and then on to Britain in February 1943. Franke was determined to be as helpful as possible to the British and spoke of his hopes of joining the British army as a cipherer, as well as expressing anti-German views. MI19 attempted to use him as a stool pigeon, but it was a dismal failure with Franke being described as 'lifeless and timid'. A stark comparison to the man who ended up in prison for a year because of speaking out against the Nazi Party. Perhaps Franke embellished some of his past a little to convince the British to use him?

Men such as Franke caused a great deal of concern in the intelligence system for the simple reason that political leanings are near enough impossible to prove. A man could be spouting anti-German sentiments, while actively spying for the Abwehr. Indeed, several British agents were doing just the reverse, fooling the Germans to trust them while reporting back to British masters. A number of captives were also clearly fanatics who jumped in with whoever was speaking to them at the time; others were trying to save their own necks by being useful, and still others had delusions of grandiose spying adventures on behalf of the British.

German deserters, in particular, drew scorn and a degree of disgust from interrogators. Lieutenant Colonel Scotland once had a POW tell him about a serious escape plot; he then allowed the rest of the betrayed plotters to enter the room and attack the traitor, only intervening after the man had suffered several blows. In Scotland's opinion it was only fitting justice for a traitor, even though the man had been helping him!

Traitors of other nationalities were viewed with greater leniency, especially men who came from conquered countries, such as Poland, Czechoslovakia and the Ukraine (to name just a few). They were seen to have a genuine and honourable reason to betray the Germans; indeed they were proving themselves loyal to their real country.

But no deliberate traitor was taken at face value, the risks were too high. All stories had to be corroborated by ISOS or other sources before anything was taken seriously, and even then the use of traitors was always done with considerable distaste.

The Man Washing his Socks

'Vitriol is an indifferent medium in which to portray a stool pigeon in any land whatever ... To call a man a spitzel, a cimbel, lokduif or a mouchoir, is worse than the casting of doubt upon the parentage of a man down Silvertown way.'[6]

Thus was the opinion of Lieutenant Colonel Stephens when it came to the use of traitors to gain information from a reticent prisoner. Stool pigeons are hardly a new idea and British intelligence knew that enemy spies would be warned against them as part of their elementary training. Stephens considered the use of such men (or women) a crude technique best avoided, as invariably the prisoner who wants to talk with a reticent inmate is suspected of being a stool pigeon. They were also often selected from men whose loyalties were uncertain and any information they obtained had to be taken with a pinch of salt and thoroughly corroborated.

Stephens wrote with his usual bluntness: 'Then when the stool pigeon fails, as almost invariably he does fail, the interrogator earns the contempt of the spy [who they have been trying to break], the investigation is irretrievably lost, the [stool pigeon] himself is blown to the rest of the prison, and an overall reticence may well affect other cases under inquiry.'

He had a point. Although he was not averse to using a stool pigeon when desperation got the better of him, they were always his last resort.

'In the ultimate, when the war is over,' he continued, stressing his case for not using stool pigeons, 'the stool pigeon blackmails the Secret Service concerned into the grant of his freedom, a pension, and ever increasing increments thereto.'

In Stephens' mind the stool pigeon was a devious traitor with no loyalty to anyone except himself. It was rather a dim view of the many men who took such a role, some voluntarily, others through coercion. Throughout POW camps, prisons and interrogation offices these stool pigeons were operating. For some it was a case of being in the wrong place at the wrong time, they knew the wrong people (or to the British, the 'right' people), they had access to important locations and meetings and, above all, they were either trusted, or deemed of so little significance that they were ignored by their fellow Germans.

For some, the suggestion of feeding the British information on other Germans was welcomed enthusiastically (indeed, some were over-enthusiastic and proved hazardous to themselves and the intelligence system), others, however, had to be press-ganged into playing the part. Stephens' sneering comments are hardly fair on these individuals who reluctantly became informants for the British.

The inevitable failure Stephens mentions was another, more serious, matter. It was one thing for the stool pigeon to despise himself for betraying his comrades, and quite another for those same comrades to learn of the betrayal. Stool pigeons had little training and within the confines of a camp or prison rumours got out. Men were spotted talking to guards, or visiting an office at odd times, and soon they were under suspicion. Depending on the nature of the men the stool pigeon betrayed, their rank and military role, he could find himself suffering a minor beating or being executed. Gestapo and SS men were the most dangerous to betray; they had no qualms about exacting revenge, rightly or wrongly.

When an escape plot at a POW camp in Comrie was discovered a man who had no involvement in the betrayal was violently attacked and killed. The real stool pigeons had not revealed their information until they were safely in a British lorry being transported to another camp. The regime of fear, which Hitler believed so effective, filtered into the prison camps and made men mistrustful of each other. The smallest sentiment of dissent against the Nazi regime could see a man swinging from a pipe in the camp latrines, and the British staff seemed unaware of the terror operating about them. For the stool pigeon, the 'despicable character', he was risking his very life to help the British, often under duress.

But there was some truth to Stephens' criticism; some authorities simply relied too heavily on prisoner informants with a detrimental effect on their usefulness.

Franz von Werra, who experienced just about every interrogation technique the British had at the time of his capture, also met an in-house stool pigeon when resident at a requisitioned mansion, Cockfosters, which the British were using as a form of interrogation/POW camp. Von Werra had proved immune to initial interrogations and had also avoided speaking and revealing information via hidden microphones (see Chapter 4), so now the British tried a different tactic. Von Werra was put in a small room with only one other occupant, a German air force leutnant who was quietly standing at a wash basin in the corner washing his socks when von Werra entered. He introduced himself to his new room-mate as Leutnant Kleinert, a pilot of the 'Schlageter' fighter *Geschwader*. Quickly becoming friendly and talkative to his new room-mate, Kleinert explained he was an Austrian who had worked as an aeronautical engineer up until a few months ago. He claimed enthusiastically to have been an assistant of the famous Professor Willi Messerschmitt and to have shook hands with all the big guns in the Luftwaffe and German Air Ministry. In fact, anyone involved in the air arms programme had apparently met with the conversational Kleinert. But it wasn't all roses for the Austrian, who von Werra noted held a deep-seated grievance against the world for all the wrongs he believed it had done to him.

Kleinert's biggest woe was how he was captured. He had been loaned to the Luftwaffe so he might fly a Messerschmitt and get first-hand experience of the aircraft in combat. On his very first operational flight his plane was shot down and he was captured.

As the famous professor's assistant, he was naturally very interested in all things Messerschmitt and as he babbled on he wanted to discuss technical matters relating to the plane with von Werra; in particular he recalled they had had problems designing the bomb racks and release mechanisms of the 109s. He wanted to know if von Werra could enlighten him on the subject.

By now von Werra was tired of the ceaseless chattering of Kleinert; he was also aware that the British wanted information on the exact things Kleinert was discussing. He coldly ordered Kleinert to be quiet, indicating the risks of hidden microphones. The Austrian laughed this off and that made von Werra even more suspicious.

Tired of games he stared directly at Kleinert and calmly noted that it was not just concealed microphones they had to fear; in fact, in that particular room they might be 'superfluous'. Flustered, Kleinert asked what he could possibly mean and with a careful psychological twist von Werra remarked that for all Kleinert knew he could be a stool pigeon. They had never met before, yet Kleinert was happy to ramble about the inner workings of a Messerschmitt; how did he know von Werra was not working for the British?

Kleinert gave the appearance of being deeply disconcerted by this remark, but brushed it off all the same as the hot workings of an overactive imagination. Still, it was not long afterwards that the Austrian was removed for interrogation and never returned.

Von Werra had his doubts about the enthusiastic Kleinert, but they would have remained unconfirmed if he had not later been taken to Grizedale Hall, one of the first POW camps. At the grand old house the new prisoners were greeted by an *Altestenrat* – a 'council of elders' overtly formed for the sole purpose of keeping camp discipline and ensuring the welfare of the men, but secretly involved in rooting out and potentially murdering suspected traitors. One U-boat captain, Leutnant Bernhard Berndt, when it was discovered at Grizedale by other officers that he had surrendered his ship, to a Hudson aircraft, on its maiden voyage was given the option of escaping from the camp that night or suffering the 'consequences'. He managed the escape but was soon caught by local Home Guard. When it became clear he was to be returned to Grizedale he broke from his captors and, despite warning shots being fired, persisted in running and was subsequently killed. To die at the hands of the British was preferable to facing the *Altestenrat* form of punishment.

It was customary for the *Altestenrat* to invite all newcomers to a meeting of prisoners in the panelled common room of Grizedale so they could discuss their experiences. It was also a subtle way of ascertaining if any of the men, if they were deemed possible traitors, required closer supervision. Von Werra was unconcerned with the attentions of the *Altestenrat* as he felt he had nothing to fear; he had, after all, resisted interrogation at every turn. He told how he was shot down and the various methods used against him to get him to talk, as he did so he came to the story about the strange Austrian Kleinert. The older inmates of Grizedale grinned and nudged one another as he spoke.

Slightly perturbed by what was so humorous, von Werra said: 'When I was taken into the room, Kleinert was ...'[7] and, as one his audience shouted back, '... standing at the wash basin, washing his socks!' Von Werra thought he was being mocked, and as the room filled with laughter, he retorted: 'You may laugh, but I'm convinced that Kleinert was never in the Luftwaffe, but is a ...' and yet again his audience filled in the blanks with '... British spy!'

It was in this way that von Werra had his suspicions about the talkative Austrian confirmed; the majority of the men at Grizedale had met the sociable Kleinert. At times he was a U-boat crewman, or the member of a bomber, or a fighter pilot, as von Werra had encountered him, but on each occasion he was always stood by the basin washing his socks when a new man arrived, as though he had been at the camp a considerable time. In short, Kleinert was a well-worn stool pigeon that the British introduced to any reticent prisoner. In fact, the Germans at Grizedale had even started using him as a way to gauge a man's loyalty. Any new prisoner who failed to mention meeting Kleinert was deemed to have fallen for the stool pigeon's antics; they would be kept under a closer watch from then on.

The case of Kleinert is a prime example of the bad use of a stool pigeon; making them a laughable tool and further producing reticence in the prisoners. No wonder that Lieutenant Colonel Stephens grumpily wrote: '... creatures of this kidney should only be used as a last resort.'[8]

Stephens might have avoided stool pigeons like the plague, but his contemporaries were more convinced of their usefulness. Guy Liddell, the director of MI5, recorded in his diaries the case of Otto Witt, in which the use of a stool pigeon created a conundrum for interrogators and saw the unfortunate Witt fall into the hands of the dubious Lieutenant Colonel Scotland.

Witt professed himself to be anti-Nazi and, to a degree, anti-German. He arrived in England under rather suspicious circumstances and with a story about having previously tried, on several occasions, to move himself into embassy circles. Witt was suspected of being a spy, but his initial interrogations resulted in no concrete information, so the case officer decided to send in a stool pigeon. This was a man by the name of Haas, who befriended Witt and was quickly taken into his confidence because he professed to be the son of a general and have a brother in the secret service.

Guy Liddell wrote in his diary on 4 March 1943: 'Witt has told the [stool pigeon] that he had been in wireless communication with Germany from Sweden, that he was at one time in touch with the Abwehr in Hamburg, that he was a member of the NSDAP and had known Reinhard Heydrich, that wireless transmission from a flat was impossible but it was as well that we should suspect him as others were doing the work. He went on to say that he was directed while in Denmark by a Gestapo announcement that he was a wanted man. He was afraid about the interrogation of his wife and of torture. Equally, he feared interrogation himself at the hands of the Czechs. He wanted to know if the fourteen spies executed had confessed, particularly "der grosse Hollander". Even if broken down, he would not give away his accomplices.'[9]

The testimony was damning, but useless. There was no real evidence to back it up and to reveal in an interrogation that Witt had spoken with a British agent would have ruined any future attempts and brought about outright denials. The chief interrogator on Witt's case was a man named Wiesner, who stated with haughty confidence that if he could be left to employ his own methods he would break the man in three days. He recommended frequent interviews at all times of the day and night to wrong-foot Witt, or, as an alternative, he would hand him to the Czechs for three days for interrogation, at the end of which he promised that Witt would return without a bruise and 'wrapped in cotton wool and silver paper'. It appears his offer was turned down.

The team, including Liddell, were stumped. They were convinced that Witt was a spy who believed in his own self-importance but was a physical coward and terrified of harsh measures. He was assumed to have built up his own standing in the SD or Gestapo eyes ('more probably the latter', remarked Liddell) and had probably volunteered to report on the activities of Otto Strauser – leader of the Black Front, a party formed of radical ex-Nazis, and a fugitive from Germany living in Canada. Goebbels called him 'Public Enemy Number One' to the Nazis and set a bounty of $500,000 on his head.

There was also debate over the truthfulness of Witt's statements, for instance, Witt had told the stool pigeon Haas that he had a *vorsatz gerat*, a device he could use for turning a receiver into a transmitter. Liddell considered this a blatant lie to bump up Witt's espionage skills in front of Haas, but one of the other case officers thought there could be truth to it. This particular officer had seen Witt, while he was under observation, carrying a heavy object out of his flat. Witt had also inferred to Haas that he had left certain apparatus with one of his accomplices.

As his confidence grew, Witt confessed to Haas that he had strong connections to the secret service and was linked to the Abwehr in Hamburg; he also expressed his terrible fear of being tortured by the Czechs should they get hold of him, though he was certain the British would not harm him. (He changed this opinion later on, as will be seen.)

The problem was that none of this amounted to a confession and it was inadmissible as evidence in a trial as it could be disproved too easily. Indeed, when Witt was eventually confronted with Haas in one interrogation and the stool pigeon ploy revealed, Witt simply denied everything. It quickly became Haas' word against his.

The stool pigeon plan had dramatically backfired. Not only was Witt denying everything, but any future attempts to get him to talk through an agent would be impossible. The game was up and the British had lost. In desperation, Witt was threatened with being handed over to the Czechs if he did not finally come clean. It was a low blow that, surprisingly (considering the British knew Witt's terrible fear of torture through Haas), hadn't been used before. With a last twist of the screw, Witt was told that if he came clean now he would face British justice, which would be an awful lot more pleasant than Czech justice. However, if he still persisted in silence then they would have no choice but to hand him to the Czech or Russian authorities. (Echoes here of Gestapo methods where a tortured subject would be suddenly confronted by a 'nice' interrogator who 'abhorred' the violent methods of his colleagues, but that if the prisoner persisted in keeping quiet then their hands were tied and he would have to be returned to the more brutal interrogators – though Witt was fairly safe, as the British did not usually follow through on such threats.)

The man who presented this ultimatum to Witt was named Victor Caroe. As soon as he told him, Witt broke down and admitted he had been lying but would now tell the truth. Caroe, however, now made the horrendous blunder of comforting Witt by telling him he did not personally think him a spy. With a few words he had once again dissolved the case and Liddell was furious; such an unthinking statement could reinforce a subject's confidence in himself. It also did Witt a disservice as Liddell decided fresh eyes and ears were needed on the case and requested that Major Scotland (later Lieutenant Colonel) take over.

Witt made the ominous journey to the London Cage on 12 March. The imposing mansion was controversial for its supposed violent methods of intelligence extraction (see Chapter 7). The idea was that Scotland would interrogate Witt until he was satisfied he had obtained all relevant information, before Witt's dreaded Czechs would be allowed in to cross-examine him. But Liddell's faith in Scotland was misplaced; he could not break Witt either, though he was convinced he was an agent of some kind. Worse, Witt would complain of mistreatment that could amount to torture, and this issue was taken seriously enough that a formal letter on the matter was sent to the Secretary of State for War.

By 18 March the interrogators had admitted defeat. Witt's case had been so badly mishandled that getting anything close to the truth from him was deemed impossible. His case was 'liquidated', though in British terms this meant shipping him to Dartmoor prison rather than marching him before a firing squad.

Guy Liddell noted in his diary: 'I am inclined to think that he is a man who has at one time or another worked for the Gestapo, that they have not got a very high regard for his ability, but that he in his conceit succeeded in persuading them to let him go and try his hand in England by investigating in political refugee circles.'[10]

Stephens could be envisaged grimacing when he heard of the disasters of his colleagues in the Witt case, not least the over-reliance and then exposure of Haas, which cost them so much. Yet even he admitted that there were certain rare occasions when a stool pigeon proved their worth. There was only ever one stool pigeon who he happily named and praised – an intellectual Brussels businessman called Johannes Ignatius Huysmans.

Huysmans was an ISOS capture, who had been traced both through his training and throughout certain missions in Britain, the USA, Brazil and Mexico. Eventually Huysmans earned a visit to the interrogators at Camp 020 while he was awaiting GIS orders in Lisbon. A secret plot between MI5, the Belgian Legation in Lisbon and the Portuguese International Police was orchestrated with Huysmans virtually wrestled onto a plane to England. Shortly after his wife was also detained and sent to Britain.

Huysmans arrived at Camp 020 bewildered by his ordeal and being referred to as an important enemy agent. Yet he was also a man of intelligence, widely travelled and fluent in five languages. Used to living under pressure he was able to maintain a mild and calm demeanour throughout his first half hour interview, politely insisting the interrogators had mistaken him for someone else.

The chink in Huysmans' armour was his wife, who he loved dearly and feared for greatly. He had been blackmailed into working for the Germans and feared reprisals against his wife; yet he was also prepared to do anything to save her. Recognising this, the camp commandant offered him a simple arrangement: talk, and the British would arrange to bring his wife to England, keep quiet and his wife would be betrayed to the Germans. It was not a particularly taxing agreement for the interrogators who knew that Mrs Huysmans was already safely in the country housed at Holloway, nor was it a tough decision for Huysmans. The spy told his story, though still lying about certain aspects and causing his interrogators to have to double-check every answer he gave. A full break was not obtained until Huysmans was told that his wife was safe, at which point he became noticeably relieved and stopped holding back.

Huysmans' tale was nothing remarkable to the officers of Camp 020. He had been blackmailed into service, but had then quite enjoyed espionage, receiving all the usual training and even being scheduled to go to England to obtain economic and military information. However, he never found a way to cross the Channel, either legally or illegally, and like so many German spies he was let down by his travel arrangements. Determined to send him somewhere, he was ordered to go to Spain and obtain a visa either for the UK or the US. His attempts failed despite being aided (or, as he might have considered it, hindered) by the local Abwehr unit. He hurried back to Amsterdam to face the wrath of his German masters.

Insisting he return to Spain and try again, Huysmans went and took his wife with him, but visa problems still hampered him and it was on this second visit that MI5 orchestrated Huysmans' kidnap and trip to England – ironic that suddenly it became so easy to travel to the UK.

Huysmans was a determined spy, who technically should have faced the death penalty. He was a dangerous man; calm under interrogation, intelligent enough to work around problems and well connected. His saving grace was that he had been shipped to Britain before he could actually commit a crime under the Treachery Act.

Huysmans had also developed, during his time in the camp, an awed impression of the British secret service, with its amazingly omnipotent powers that enabled it to snatch his wife from the clutches of the Germans. He willingly offered his own services to the camp and became the only stooge Stephens showed any respect for.

He had a natural talent for acting as a counsellor to reticent prisoners. Without expecting pay or any other promises, governed only by the hope he might one day leave the camp alive and with his wife, he set about quietly unravelling the stories of his fellow internees.

Huysmans approach was nothing less than ingenious. Unlike the usual stool pigeon who tried to extract information, Huysmans refused to listen to another man's story. He presented himself as a man full of woe, with the weight of the world on his shoulders. He never knew the stories behind the men he was put with, and that added natural sincerity to any conversations they had; he was also viewed as being worldly wise and a good man for giving advice.

Huysmans would always begin by telling his own story from start to finish, including the magic powers of the British in sweeping his wife from the Germans, and their fairness in his treatment. He would then go away and not return until the prisoner asked for him. When this happened the case officers would play a dangerous game of sometimes refusing the first request to make the situation seem more authentic. They would desperately hope the request would be repeated and it often was.

Even then, Huysmans did not make life easy for his victims. He would tell them quite plainly: 'I do not wish to listen to your story; I have too much trouble of my own. All I can say for myself is that I am alive.'

This reluctance would usually have the prisoner begging Huysmans to listen and help, desperate for him to advise them on what to do. Should they talk? Should they tell the whole truth? Huysmans kept up his dour appearance, before answering: 'The responsibility is too great. All I can say is that I spoke the truth, they checked every word of it – and I am alive.'

Eventually the interrogators would receive a little note from the Brussels businessman along the lines of: 'Number […] is, I think, ready to talk. Perhaps he will react to sympathy, this one, rather than to heavy interrogation. It is for you, honoured Sir, to decide. I do not know his case.'

Huysmans ranks as one of the few successful stool pigeons used among the interrogators. He was never found out, never even suspected, but in part that was due to the interrogators' sparse use of his skills and their dedication to keeping him a secret. Stephens knew the risks of revealing all his tricks; he only had to look at the examples of his colleagues to see why.

Huysmans earned his freedom, a prize he might have otherwise been denied. Yet it is not surprising that his name was the only one Stephens ever mentioned and that Camp 020 rarely used him. The usefulness of traitors was always a debatable subject.

Notes

1 A 1965 statement by Fritz Kolbe, as reprinted in 'Germany finally honours the "traitor" who gave Nazi secrets to America', *The Independent*, Saturday, 25 September 2004.
2 Lieutenant Colonel Stephens (ed.), *A Digest of Ham*.
3 Interrogation files held at The National Archives, WO208/4117-4197.
4 Ibid.
5 Ibid.
6 Lieutenant Colonel Stephens (ed.), *A Digest of Ham*.
7 Kendal Burt & James Leasor, *The One that Got Away*.
8 Lieutenant Colonel Stephens (ed.), *A Digest of Ham*.
9 Nigel West (ed.), *The Guy Liddell Diaries: 1942–1945, Vol 2*, Routledge, 2005.
10 Ibid.

5

MASTERS OF THE MICROPHONE

The world of hidden microphones is familiar to any person who has seen a spy drama, or read a thriller, or even followed newspaper reports on tapped phone lines. 'Bugs' are the cliché of espionage. Rooms being searched for devices either by a James Bond character or a black-suited FBI man is a classic scene in the popular media image of espionage yet, like so much of British intelligence, the bug really only proved its worth in the Second World War.

The microphone, though now such a standard piece of modern technology, was still a relatively new device as war broke out. The creator of the microphone is usually named as Emile Berliner, who, in 1876, created a new transmitter to improve the recently invented telephone. Two years later David Edward Hughes developed the carbon microphone, versions of which are still used today. However, it was the growing popularity of radio that spurred on further microphone developments, in particular the condenser microphone in the 1920s. This subsequently led to the development of a system with the ability to record sound to film – an advancement that would first have impact on the popular media of the day, but later would have significant effects on the war effort.

After recording, the next step was to design smaller microphones that could be handheld, as well as microphones that were multi-directional, enabling a wider usage. Reliability and better sound quality were other considerations that were driven by the expansion of radio use. By the 1930s the mike had moved on from its early unreliable, crackly form to a superior recording device.

The development can be starkly seen in the difference of 'bugging' between both world wars. In the First World War Lieutenant Colonel Scotland, when wishing to record a prisoner's interview, stationed several officers with notebooks around the outside corners of a tent to write down what they heard. They were human microphones and the walls, quite literally, had ears. Fast forward less than thirty years and Lieutenant Colonel Stephens' listeners were stationed in separate rooms with microphones linked to recording reels, thus replacing the human ears.

Yet the use of microphones was still in its infancy. People would rapidly learn during those war years of the dangers of listening devices, and even at the start they were treated with a certain degree of suspicion and secrecy.

The Mysterious 'M'

When Stephens wrote in *A Digest of Ham* about the use of microphones, he was clearly still concerned about the risks of revealing too much about this tactical tool. So wary was he of saying too much about the devices employed at Camp 020, that only once in his section on microphone cover did he use the actual word; on all other occasions it is referred to as 'M', 'M' cover, 'M' staff or 'M' operators.

At this early stage of the world of microphone espionage, the extent in which secret listening devices would be used in later years had not been envisioned. Telephone taps, minuscule electronic bugs and devices that can turn a phone into a transmitter were science fiction ideas of the future. For Stephens' team, the microphone was still a relatively bulky device that required discretion in placement and vast teams for collating the information it produced. In fact the microphone was, initially at least, badly handled in many cases and used in rather a limited manner.

'In the early stages of the war, "M" was used in a very unscientific manner, being operated almost entirely by interrogators who, immediately after interrogation, would listen in and endeavour to assess whether their PW had told the truth or not.'[1]

The benefits of microphones were simply not recognised. Some interrogators even viewed them uncomfortably, seeing them as a way to contradict or 'check up on' the case officers. Successes obtained during the Blitz, however, dispelled these doubts, at least in the minds of the senior officers, and the microphone department was developed into a more co-ordinated and organised part of the interrogation system. A permanent workforce was engaged to solely work on listening to the microphones and transcribing useful information that came through. It was far from an easy or 'soft' job. A lot of responsibility rested on the 'M' operators' shoulders, more so than that of the interrogators in some instances.

They were the backup for every interview; the men and women the interrogators relied on when prisoners were reticent or lying. It was not enough for the operators to just have a good grounding in languages (though obviously it was an essential component); they also had to have good background knowledge on both the cases at hand and the wartime politics. Added to this was the need for a flair for being able to filter out useful information from that which was more mundane – not a simple task considering the extent of seemingly 'pointless' details the interrogators liked to keep. Who would have thought, after all, that a lion cub named Simba could be a key fact when it came to the interrogation of a German flying ace?

Of around 200 officers and other ranks who worked in the microphone room during the war, only a dozen were considered exemplary and even they could make serious mistakes. Ironically, matters grew worse as the interrogators began to realise the benefits of having their interviews recorded. Interrogators started to rely too heavily on the microphones and were anxious to have all their dealings with prisoners listened in to. The burden on the 'M' department was too great and it became necessary to insist that only the most important interrogations should be covered.

Most interrogation centres started to incorporate hidden microphones into all their holding cells. Considering the bulkiness of the technology this was no easy feat, yet the resourcefulness of those placing the microphones overcame most obstacles and enabled a team of listeners to monitor the rooms from early morning to midnight. In special cases it was considered prudent to monitor the prisoner for twenty-four hours, but most were allowed to sleep without surveillance.

Teamwork between interrogators and 'M' operators was essential, though it took time for the former to trust those men and women who were listening in. Resentment, especially when a statement an interrogator had extracted from a prisoner was contradicted outright by an 'M' operator, hampered early relations, as did mistrust in the equipment. In a modern age when so much unequivocal confidence is placed in recording devices, whether it is a video camera, tape recorder or even a mobile phone, it can seem hard to imagine the consternation the introduction of microphones caused to interrogators. But there was anger and dislike towards this inanimate device that seemed to be suggesting the interrogators were unreliable and needed as much monitoring as the prisoners. Interrogators were somewhat of a breed apart in the army and they required a great deal of self-confidence to be successful. This self-confidence could sometimes come across as arrogance; they didn't like being told they were wrong.

Despite initial tensions, it did not take long for all aspects of the interrogation system to realise the benefits of using microphones. Close liaison between the two teams was fundamental to success. It soon became an unwritten rule at Camp 020, for instance (and no doubt elsewhere as well), that an interrogator never began an interview without first consulting with the 'M' operator who was monitoring his particular prisoner. This ensured that the interrogator did not interrupt an interesting conversation the operator might be listening to. Important points of interest that the interrogator was trying to ascertain from the suspect were also discussed, so the 'M' operator would be able to keep an ear open should the prisoner start talking about them when he returned to his cell. This was all part of the interrogators' psychological ploys and very often an interview was more about priming a suspect for later microphone coverage in his cell, than to actually gain information direct. The device proved successful when it came to a number of reluctant prisoners, though more savvy agents were quick to recognise the risks of hidden microphones.

'M' coverage also revealed instances when a POW held unexpected intelligence that otherwise would never have come to the attention of the interrogators. One such instance was that of a prisoner sent to be interrogated on his expert knowledge of diesel engines. He was kept in solitary confinement for five weeks while British technical experts picked his brains on the subject, before finally being placed with other prisoners. The operators kept up their usual cover and were rewarded when, within hours of being placed with other men, the prisoner revealed that he knew a great deal about the secret V-weapons the Germans were developing. These potentially devastating weapons had kept the British military authorities awake at night and any nugget of information was valuable. By the use of hidden microphones it was revealed that the diesel expert held quite a few of these useful nuggets and he subsequently provided details of both the V-1 and V-2 weapons a full year before the weapons were ever used.

In a similar case a survivor of the sinking of the German battlecruiser *Scharnhorst* was routinely monitored by 'M'. The sinking of the *Scharnhorst*, though a heavy blow to the Germans and a triumph of a carefully co-ordinated British ambush, was not of particular intelligence value. However, while being observed the prisoner revealed that he had previously served on the *Tirpitz*, a sister ship to the *Scharnhorst*. The pair of cruisers had been sailing to Arctic Norway to harass Russia-bound convoys, when British midget submarines badly damaged the *Tirpitz* and sent her limping away abandoning the *Scharnhorst*. Up until that point the British had not been able to obtain an eye-witness account from the German side of this particular attack; it was a vital piece of missing intelligence that could help them to hone the midget submarines' attacks in the future. Without the hidden microphones it would never have been realised by the interrogators that the prisoner they had lost interest in could actually prove so useful.

There were other instances, too numerous to recount, when a recorded conversation exposed that the Germans were using new inventions of which the British knew nothing. Often even the prisoner was not aware of how secret these devices must have been and innocently talked about them with a colleague. Without access to these 'private' conversations British intelligence would have been in the dark.

In other ways the 'M' department proved its worth. It was the only way to check on the truthfulness of the information supplied by German or Italian stool pigeons who, as mentioned above, were regarded with deep distrust. The existence of escape plans was another problem regularly rooted out by operators listening in.

Then there was the welfare aspect. At Camp 020 the operators were expected to report on the attitudes of the warders to the prisoners. Lieutenant Colonel Stephens was adamant that his staff should not resort to violence at any time and he would check on them to ensure this.

Lastly, the microphones provided a trusted source for listening to outside Allied officers who might enter the camp to interrogate a suspect. Most interrogation centres, by their very nature, are a closed community and an outsider coming in was an occasion for distrust and anxiety. If such an intruder managed to obtain permission to see a prisoner alone then the odds of that officer reporting what he had learned were slim. Hidden microphones in the interrogation room were the only means of ascertaining what had been said. It is sad that in a time of war such methods had to be taken with allies, but secrecy and distrust tends to be infectious and outside of familiar circles everyone was suspect.

Microphones almost came to be seen as a wonder device, an infallible way of obtaining information, but because of their efficiency they became costly. They were over-relied on in certain cases and interrogators could neglect using direct interrogation, believing the microphones would catch everything in time. It could almost be viewed as a form of laziness that the interrogators fell into; content to leave their work to a recorded conversation and a man with headphones. They had to be reminded on occasion that they still had a job to do.

Yet more hazardous to the use of listening devices was exposure; it did not take many years for the use of hidden microphones to become such common knowledge that prisoners began to prove themselves 'mike-conscious'. Even as early as 1940, certain astute German captives realised the danger.

Franz von Werra's adventures in England have already been mentioned, not least because his observations of those who observed him would forever change the way Germans viewed British interrogation (and also made him the last person our government and military wanted to successfully escape back to Germany). Aside from direct and indirect interrogations and stool pigeons, he was treated to an episode with hidden microphones.

It began at Trent Park, Cockfosters. Von Werra was proving an irritation to the British interrogators and they were finally sick of his evasions; their attempts became distinctly less subtle and roused the suspicions of the already wary fighter ace.

Upon being brought to an interrogation room von Werra was cordially asked if he would like to be moved to a room with other prisoners. Up until this point von Werra had been kept largely isolated, the usual ploy of the interrogators to prevent information being shared among the POWs and also to engender a desire to talk through sheer lack of opportunity. Nonetheless, von Werra greeted the suggestion noncommittally. The interrogator, endeavouring to be agreeably affable, said he would read out a list of

Bad Nenndorf, once a prosperous spa resort, became the location for the most notorious Allied interrogation camp.

Das ist der Staffel-Löwe Simba

Franz von Werra, the famous escapee, is pictured here on a German magazine. It was this image that gave away his identity to the British.

To avoid serious interrogation or risk of torture it was best to be a low-ranking soldier. This young man should have had nothing to fear from the London Cage.

Husband and wife spy teams occasionally came through the doors of Camp 020. In each case it was usually the man who broke first.

Grizedale was an early interrogation camp, which famously held Franz von Werra. It has subsequently been demolished.

Every soldier that came through British hands was routinely questioned; exceptions were only made by error. There was no telling who could hold vital information so everyone was interviewed.

German harbours (especially ones where U-boats moored) were constantly on the interrogators' wish list of things to learn about.

Pre-war German athletics and training fascinated the British. These two pictures would have baffled them; they never quite understood the German focus on sporting prowess.

See below left.

This is an American interrogating a German. The photo is staged for the press, but the habit of showing photos to a suspect was common enough. British and American interrogators worked closely together.

Loose Talk can cost Lives!

Anyone connected with U-boats was of especial interest to the British, as they were desperate to find ways to stop the destruction to convoys.

This famous saying, illustrated here by a man listening to a secret conversation, was actually used to advertise Stetsons in America during the war. The tagline is 'Keep it under your Stetson', but the message itself was vitally important.

PUB
TELF

"...sails tonight, world's biggest, packed with troops...Berlin waiting"

German military movements were regularly wrung out of prisoners to buy the Allies time, or even to get them ahead.

Lower-ranking U-boat crew were still of interest as they may have had some dealings with the Enigma machine, which the British needed to break to win the war.

Officers, if not willing to talk, were often put into communal cells with men of their own rank. They were then listened to with the aid of microphones to see if they let anything slip.

Spies came to Britain in all manner of ways, including crossing the Channel by boat – though generally they would not fly a flag to broadcast their intentions.

Officers were held responsible for the crimes of their men and could end up in the hands of Lieutenant Colonel Scotland.

Agents often parachuted into England, but were routinely rounded up. Intelligence was familiar with the practice having witnessed it in the First World War, as demonstrated here.

Lieutenant Colonel Scotland spent the First World War questioning men like these, an experience that would give him good grounding for his Second World War work.

In both wars suspect civilians were interned and interrogated for treachery. Here, men camp in tents waiting their turn.

The pre-war threat posed by Germany scared many. This picture, taken in 1933, is a portentous image. MI5, however, were more concerned with communists.

Young sailors share sweets before leaving. Going to sea was risky enough, but if you had the misfortune of being on a U-boat that was sunk you had a less than 50% chance of survival.

The Abwehr, one of Germany's secret services, used threats to family to recruit agents. It was a ploy that made spies easy to turn.

British interrogators also used tacit threats to one's family, or sometimes promises to help get them to Britain, to persuade men and women to talk.

When soldiers were captured in a group it didn't matter if one refused to talk, others were bound to be more loose-tongued.

The stereotypical look of a spy – yet the best spies were inconspicuous and could blend into a crowd. Of course, these coats and suits were commonplace at the time.

Is he spying? It was a question that every civilian asked themselves when they spotted something suspicious. Later in the war, the intelligence services took no chances and arrested any suspects.

Oath-breakers were seen to be the worst kind of traitors. Here, young men eager to fight in the First World War hold up Bibles to swear loyalty to the Crown.

A Tiger tank in the Ardennes. One of the most feared pieces of German equipment, the British made little headway when interrogating on the subject.

A radio operator taps in messages. Men like this were often the first to be interviewed as signal sending was such a vital part of the counter-espionage and war effort.

It was men like these that Lieutenant Colonel Scotland served beside, was betrayed by, and ultimately interrogated.

Oath-breakers were seen to be the worst kind of traitors. Here, young men eager to fight in the First World War hold up Bibles to swear loyalty to the Crown.

A Tiger tank in the Ardennes. One of the most feared pieces of German equipment, the British made little headway when interrogating on the subject.

A Tiger tank in action; a rotating cupola and lockable tracks for quick turning made the Tiger a formidable vehicle to fight.

Tank crew death rates were appalling; when the machine was destroyed it often took the men inside with it. This made finding sufficient men to interrogate on the subject extremely difficult.

A U-boat crew jubilant before a mission. The devastation they wreaked on Allied convoys reached a peak during the Battle of the Atlantic.

Interrogators desperately wanted to know where U-boats were being moored so they could launch a strike. Most prisoners were, however, tight-lipped on the matter.

A radio operator taps in messages. Men like this were often the first to be interviewed as signal sending was such a vital part of the counter-espionage and war effort.

It was men like these that Lieutenant Colonel Scotland served beside, was betrayed by, and ultimately interrogated.

prisoner names and all von Werra needed to do was nod when he recognised a name and it would be arranged for him to be moved into the same room. It was far too obvious that this was yet another trick, though von Werra was not certain what the motivation was. He speculated the British had captured men who were refusing to give the name of their unit, so they were running the names past von Werra to see if he recognised them. Another possibility was that a man had lied, claiming to know von Werra, and they were testing this. Whatever the reason, von Werra maintained his stony calm and did not move his head a fraction even though he knew most of the men named.

Exasperated, yet again the interrogator's affable veneer faltered. He complained that von Werra was being stupid and unreasonable, but that, despite it all, he would live up to their agreement and put von Werra in a room with a comrade – who would he prefer?

Von Werra stubbornly held his tongue on the subject, only answering that any German would do. Angered, the interrogator declared he would be put in a room with a certain leutnant who was deemed 'queer in the head' and that maybe that experience would make him more reasonable to answering questions.

Von Werra was marched to a different room. The interrogator unlocked the door and went inside and then the ace fighter pilot was ushered in. To his complete surprise the man inside the room was not the 'queer in the head' leutnant that had been mentioned but Oberleutnant Carl Westerhoff, not only a Luftwaffe comrade but an old and close friend. To von Werra it was obvious that this was yet another test and he tried to keep up a façade of not knowing Westerhoff by clicking his heels and greeting him like a stranger. But it was no good; in the end von Werra could not compensate for human emotion and Westerhoff was too ecstatic to see his friend. It later turned out that Westerhoff had previously been as tight-lipped as von Werra and had refused to give his unit. He had also been one of the few pilots who took the precaution of setting fire to their crashed plane and burning their papers. The British had therefore been gambling on von Werra knowing him and thus revealing that he was a *Geschwader* (squadron) comrade.

Yet that was only the start of the ruse. Westerhoff did not have a cynical caution of von Werra and wanted to talk and learn all about what had happened to his friend after crashing in England. This, again, was what the interrogators were gambling on. The casual chatter could lead to vital information.

Von Werra, with his honed suspicions, recognised the danger and shushed his comrade: 'There's bound to be a microphone in this room somewhere. Let's look for it. That ventilator grille in the corner, first. I'll climb up on to your shoulders and have a look. Don't say anything!'[2]

Westerhoff showed a natural disbelief, which the British played on so well, but he followed the instructions and von Werra discovered the hidden microphone in the grille. It was difficult to see, but he could make out a black object and wires, so he was certain he was correct. He thought it best that both comrades should talk, leaning out of the window in future to avoid being heard.

'The British didn't put us together for nothing,' Von Werra remarked dryly. From then on incriminating conversations were held out the window or, if it was night and the blackout shutter was up, they removed themselves to a remote corner and spoke there. The rest of the time they talked about mundane topics and even developed a game of inventing fictitious Germans, including their hobbies, girlfriends, military adventures and appearances for the benefit of the British.

Von Werra might have felt cocky and self-assured in this new game of fooling the inferior British, but his interrogators were to have the last laugh. His elation at finding the microphone and striking another blow at his captors had masked a nagging doubt in his mind that only resurfaced on the third day in the room. It was then that it dawned on him what was wrong with the placement of the microphone – it was too obvious. He could imagine his fellow Germans back home hiding a device in such a manner, but not the British who were more subtle in these matters. The thought troubled him. Supposing the British had meant for it to be obvious? Supposing it was a set up?

Once he began to think like that the rest of the awful truth slowly fell into place. There was the window for a start. In every other room the window had been screwed shut to prevent prisoners escaping or committing suicide, but it seemed in this one cell such a possibility had been overlooked. The window being able to be opened made it the obvious place to lean out of and talk to avoid a secret mike. And hadn't his interrogator stood right in front of the window when he first entered the room? Could that have been another subtle trick to direct his attentions from a second microphone?

Westerhoff was baffled by this sudden revelation, as von Werra babbled to him: 'Eight chaps out of ten would look for a microphone as soon as they were moved into the room, and find it, as we did, in the first half an hour. Having found it, they would feel so pleased with their cleverness that it would never occur to them, as it has only occurred to me when it's too late, that they were being deliberately tricked into talking into another properly concealed mike, outside the window!'[3]

Von Werra followed this statement by making a thorough search of the window frame, but try as he might no microphone could be found. As he searched he spoke a running commentary to the people he believed were listening to him. After the fruitless search it was perhaps somewhat more than coincidental that both Westerhoff and von Werra were immediately removed from the room and separated.

Von Werra was perhaps unduly harsh in his thinking that if Germans used hidden microphones they would hide them in the most obvious place. In the early stages of the war, when the art of listening in by microphone was a new novelty, he might have had a case. But the Germans too realised that prisoners were becoming savvier to listening devices. They came against the same problems as the British. The example of Michel Bernin demonstrates this plainly.

Before the war, Bernin was a French film producer and a member of the naval reserve. Called up in 1939 to serve as a French navy photographer he was involved in a number of adventures, and survived Dunkirk, but was captured by the Nazis at Cherbourg. He was sent to the ancient fortress of Konigstein for his internment, before eventually being released and allowed to go to America in 1942.

Konigstein seems to have been rife with microphones but, at least initially, this was not a concern for Bernin who was too busy serving as an orderly to Admiral Leclerc. He would not have found the first hidden microphone in the admiral's room had it not been for a stroke of fortune. One of the buttons on Admiral Leclerc's jacket had cracked from use and fallen off. Bernin knew it would be impossible to replace and as 'keeping up appearances' was such an important part of resisting the Germans, even in prison, he spent some time searching for it, before realising it had rolled under the bed.

Bernin went to move the bed and was surprised to find that it was fixed to the wall. Unperturbed, he crawled under the bed where he found the button and something else: a large black microphone. Admiral Leclerc was becoming impatient and started to ask what was the matter. Bernin crawled back out with a finger to his lips, then, quietly, he walked to a table in the room where a paper and pencil had been left. He wrote carefully: 'Under the bed, near the wall, there is a microphone!'[4]

The admiral was suitably stunned. He went to the bed and looked under for himself, and when he arose his expression was blank: 'This coffee is cold,' he said to Bernin, but directing his words to the position of the mike. 'Next time try to bring me warm coffee.'[5]

Bernin, realising the deception, responded with a similar mundane comment about bringing fresher coffee, then the admiral motioned that they should step outside the room: '"To hell with these German methods!" He exclaimed, "It was a lucky chance that you [Bernin] discovered the microphone." After reflecting a moment he added, "Unfortunately three days have already passed during which our jailers have had complete knowledge of our most confidential conversations."'[6]

Franz von Werra, and no doubt British intelligence as well, would have been unimpressed that such an obvious microphone had been missed by the admiral. But it goes to show that, at least in the early days of war, secret surveillance was not recognised for the danger it was. It is also interesting to note that such clandestine observation was deemed by the admiral as a 'German method' and rather under-handed, perhaps not something the Allies would stoop to!

Now that the first microphone had been found at Konigstein, word quickly spread and the prisoners became, as the British termed it, mike-conscious. Efforts were made to discover how thorough the Germans had been with their installation of listening devices. The various French officers held in the prison started a systematic search of rooms and corridors. The first outside microphone was found at the far end of a corridor just underneath a bulletin board where the prison commandant posted news and information. Disheartened, the prisoners realised this meant he had been able to hear any comments or criticisms they had made about the notices he posted.

The extent of the surveillance now had everyone feeling deeply paranoid. At 9.30 a.m. it was part of the prison routine for all the officers to be allowed to walk around the castle park. Though surrounded by wire, the garden, which largely constituted a grove of trees, was a pleasant excursion from the cells of the old fortress. It was intersected by paths and in the centre a pleasant clearing had been made with a bench to encourage strollers to sit and rest. It was the sort of place that would inspire relaxation and casual conversation.

Bernin, as an orderly, was not allowed to go into the park except for an hour on Sundays. He watched with dread from a window as the officers strolled and talked. It seemed obvious to him that the park would be a prime place for the Germans to hide microphones (it is also striking that Bernin had such low regard for his officers' intelligence that he assumed they would be unable to deduce this for themselves).

The first two generals to return from their walk were the French war hero Giraud and his closest friend Prioux. Bernin approached Giraud frantically, telling them his theory about microphones in the garden and adding, 'Possibly you did not think of this.'

Giraud laughed at him, despite the insubordination, and explained laboriously: 'Yes, indeed we did [think about microphones]. We thought very much about it. The microphones between the branches transmitted today to the Germans the first lecture on military history by General Champon. It was a very brilliant lecture about German defeats from Charlemagne to 1918. The Germans were also taught – in case they were ignorant of the fact – that this castle Konigstein has housed generals before. That was in 1813, in Napoleon's time, when one of the army chiefs of the emperor, General Vandannes, chose this castle for his headquarters during his campaign in Prussia ...'[7]

Just like von Werra's game of inventing Germans for the benefit of the British 'M' operators, the French officers had enjoyed belittling their enemy through a history lecture. The Germans were irritated that their extensive network of microphones now seemed to be almost useless; they resorted to more typical tactics, including trying to induce the orderlies to spy on their officers. One man was instructed in an interview to discover which of the officers favoured collaboration with Germany and which where pro-British. When he politely refused, he was informed that they had taken hostages from Brest, where he lived, which included his father. It was intimated that, should he fail to help the Germans, a bullet would find its way into his father.

The orderly, as the Germans expected, felt compelled to agree. Blackmail was a common tactic for recruiting spies, but it always left a patriotic man feeling dishonoured and disgusted with himself. This inevitably led to them seeking to talk about the situation and provide information to the Allies.

Such was the case with the orderly, who reported what had happened to a French general and from then on was given fictitious reports to feed back to his German 'masters'.

The misuse of microphones (or, perhaps more appropriately, the misplacement) could ruin what might otherwise have been a very significant espionage tool. Back in Britain, at Camp 020 it was recognised that more and more POWs were arriving mike-conscious and immediately set about looking for bugs when they were left in their cells. Fortunately, if the microphones were not discovered this conscientiousness usually evaporated after a few days. There was a misguided impression among the men that the danger of surveillance only existed in the first hour or so after an initial interrogation. After that it was believed they were free from being overheard and many could not resist the temptation to talk to their comrades on wartime topics.

The longer prisoners remained at a certain camp, the more likely they would eventually slip up and begin talking on subjects the British hoped to overhear. Suitable news reports, magazine articles or stool pigeons would be introduced to certain prisoners to spark a conversation. Anything that generated an argument was usually good for the 'M' operators as, when the debate became heated, the men often forgot to hold their tongues.

It has to be remembered, of course, that not all men had the suspicious and cunning mind of Franz von Werra, or the astute senses of Michel Bernin. Some didn't recognise the risk of observation; others did not even believe it existed. Some simply failed to realise that the information they held was either secret or important, and then there were the men who just couldn't resist talking and never knew when to keep quiet. Among these men the microphone was most effective. Camp 020 did not have a microphone department for nothing, and while certain suspects had the intellect to elude them, many more chattered away oblivious to the men and women listening in.

When used properly the hidden microphones could be of extreme strategic value. When the war concluded there was a new rush to collect information from the Nazis, particularly on scientific theories or weapon development. One of the biggest concerns of the Allies was the nuclear technology the Germans had invented. The Nazis regularly fed a stream of rumours as part propaganda on 'new' weapons, but the truth behind them could be difficult to ascertain. As the Nazi regime fell, Britain and America made a decision to ensure the foremost physicists working for the Nazi Party, when captured, were sent to England. This was largely to avoid them falling into Russian hands, at least until America had had the chance to win the atomic race and detonate the first bomb.

The detention site was to be a quiet little manor house in Cambridge, East Anglia, called Farm Hall. For a brief six months at the end of the war it became home and prison for ten of Germany's top nuclear scientists.

'At Farm Hall each of [the prisoners] was assigned a prisoner-of-war batman to look after his needs. There was a tennis court and a piano for Heisenberg. The bedrooms were panelled and the food good. What none of them seem to have realised, at least initially, was that [the] estate had been wired to record conversations.'[8]

The interrogators worked on the theory that direct examination would not produce the full answers they needed to their biggest question, namely what had happened to the Germans' nuclear programme – why had they failed to build the bomb? The rigging of the house by MI6 with listening devices was considered the best solution. The house was secluded and cosy, with many comforts that had probably not been experienced for some time. Their lifestyle was, indeed, probably better than what they would have faced had they not been captured, and this atmosphere produced a generalised ease in the prisoners that was conducive to conversation. There was also the hope that by just being together the scientists could not help but talk about their work with each other. The desire to confer and compare notes would, it was felt, be just too great.

Even so, it was the dramatic events at Hirsoshima that truly sparked the scientists into discussing the Nazi atomic programme. Listening to a BBC radio report on the Hiroshima bombing in their cosy country retreat, they were suddenly stunned back to the reality of war.

The catastrophic explosion opened the floodgates as the German physicists gasped in awe that the Allies had achieved what they could not. The microphone operators listened keenly as the scientists began to debate the reasons why their own atomic programme had lagged behind. The brilliant theorist Heisenberg (who would later win a Nobel Prize for physics in 1944 and campaign adamantly against the use of nuclear weapons) expressed intense disbelief at the news and dismissed it as propaganda. After all, his team had been working for years on the project and had achieved nothing. Another physicist, Hahn, took the news at face value, even though it destroyed him to think how his discovery of uranium fission had resulted in such an apocalyptic weapon.

Aside from the factual evidence MI6 was looking for, which its operators were keenly transcribing, the microphones picked up a psychological tension among the scientists – a tension that turned into defensiveness that in turn sparked the scientists to begin talking about 'moral superiority' and its role in their failure to create an atomic bomb.

One of the physicists, Weizsacker, stated: 'I believe we didn't do it [create the atomic bomb] because all the physicists didn't want to do it, on principle. If we had all wanted Germany to win the war we would have succeeded … History will record that the Americans and the English made a bomb, and that at the same time the Germans, under the Hitler regime, produced a workable machine [critical reactor]. In other words, the peaceful development of the uranium machine was made in Germany under the Hitler regime, whereas the Americans and the English developed this ghastly weapon of war.'[9]

It was not quite what MI6 had expected from its bugs, that the German physicists would start to suggest they had maintained the moral high ground over the Allies. In fact, what the microphones were picking up was the mental gymnastics of men horrified by their part in the war, their part in mass destruction, and the psychological twists and turns they were endeavouring to make in their own heads to ease their consciences. Above all else they wanted to believe they would not have built a bomb.

Though some believed this, the more cynical (and most intelligence officers and interrogators fell into this category) were more interested in the practical reasons why the Germans had failed.

The recordings from Farm Hall revealed the down-to-earth reasons behind the lack of success, as Heisenberg said: 'We just couldn't. Anything we might have done, to separate isotopes would have been a very big enterprise which we simply could not afford with all the other pressures of the war. And also if we had built a big factory, it would have been bombed.'[10]

It seems Heisenberg may also have suffered from a misunderstanding of atomic theory. After the bomb had exploded at Hiroshima, his colleagues asked him to give a talk on critical mass. Heisenberg presented a talk that made no sense (and which was all recorded by the eager 'M' operators). His talk was based on building a reactor, a fundamentally different process to building a bomb. He realised his error a week later and revised his theory and presented another, correct talk on the matter.

The recordings from Farm Hall, which have now been transcribed and published, cast a damning light on the physicists, producing the sort of evidence interrogators dream of. In all early conversations there had been evidence that the scientists could not build a bomb for practical reasons (funding, manpower and incorrect designs) not because of moral doubts. Only after Hiroshima did that idea surface. In direct interrogation there would have been more danger of the men becoming defensive earlier on, but by listening in surreptitiously the real truth was visible. The microphone had achieved what direct confrontation probably would not have and, in the decades that have followed the war, our secret service, as well as private parties, have learned the benefits of leaving a microphone on when people don't know and when their guard is down.

However, as this chapter has shown, the secret of hidden microphones – if they ever could be considered much of a secret – did not last long at all. Very rapidly spies, soldiers and civilians realised the risks of bugs and the advantage was partially lost.

In Germany, where an atmosphere of constant surveillance had produced deep-set paranoia in many, the fear of hidden microphones was extremely prevalent.

'No one – if he were not foolish – said or did anything that might be interpreted as "anti-Nazi" without first taking precautions that it was not being recorded by hidden SD [Sicherheitsdienst] microphones or overheard by an SD agent.'[11]

The idea that the very walls had ears had arrived and anyone with any sense avoided talking about sensitive topics unless in a safe place. No wonder then that Franz von Werra was so alert to the possibility of bugs, but the British knew this and used it against him and others. Dummy microphones boosted morale in POWs, gave them confidence, made them cocky and, ultimately, opened their mouths.

The world of interrogation and surveillance would never be the same once listening devices became common practice. But for all their dismal connotations of Orwell's *1984* and Big Brother watching our every movement, the microphone did enable the British to learn secrets that otherwise would have remained concealed. It was an overused tool, in some cases so badly placed that it ruined any hope of obtaining information, but when cunningly hidden it could reveal more than the truth from a POW; it could reveal their fears, their hopes, their weaknesses. It could teach interrogators how to turn the screw on a man and how to break him. It could expose liars and it could be used to monitor new interrogators and even camp staff. Ultimately, no one was exempt from its scope.

Aside from stool pigeons (which, as has been seen, were widely distrusted) the microphone was the only real means of catching a man off guard in conversation. The use of such a device was always viewed with a tinge of discomfort, a feeling that it was 'below the belt'. But it worked, it saved Britain, it broke traitors and it exposed secrets. Without it, Britain's interrogators would have missed vital information and that information could not then have been passed on to the intelligence services. It was simple. It was subtle. Perhaps, it could even be argued, it won the war. But it has left us with a feeling that we should always be looking over our shoulders (or, at least, checking under the bed for microphones). After all, the familiar poster summed it up on every street of Britain: 'Careless Talk Costs Lives!' And that was one thing the interrogators knew all too well.

Notes
1 Lieutenant Colonel Stephens (ed.), *A Digest of Ham*.
2 Kendal Burt & James Leasor, *The One that Got Away*.
3 Ibid.
4 Michel Bernin, 'Konigstein Prison', in *Life*, 21 September 1942.
5 Ibid.
6 Ibid.
7 Ibid.
8 Jeremy Bernstein, *Hitler's Uranium Club: The Secret Recordings at Farm Hall*, Springer, 2001.
9 Mary Palevsky, *Atomic Fragments: A Daughter's Questions*, University of California Press, 2000.
10 Ibid.
11 Frederik Nebeker, *Dawn of the Electronic Age: Electrical Technologies in the Shaping of the Modern World, 1914 to 1945*, Wiley-Blackwell, 2009.

6

TIGER TANKS
AND ENIGMA MACHINES:
THE GREAT SUCCESSES
AND THE DISASTROUS FAILURES

There were numerous key moments in the war that shaped its progress, some better remembered than others. Behind every success, every skilled attack, every elaborate ploy, was a wealth of intelligence drawn from a range of sources, including the stalwart interrogators. Throughout the war various topics haunted military and government minds, and for each one the intelligence network went to work, not least by making a point of capturing and interrogating the most useful of people.

Of course, the necessity to follow every reliable rumour could sometimes lead to confusion and failure. In late 1940 there was the strange episode of *Fall funfundachtzig*, loosely translated as the Eighty-Fives Scare. Rumours had surfaced about a secret project called *die Funfundachtziger* – the Eighty-Fives, but no one knew anymore than the name. POWs were suddenly bombarded with urgent questions on the subject. Subtle techniques were thrown out the window and prisoners were repeatedly hauled to an interview room and asked the same question, 'What are the Eighty-Fives?' The prisoners had no answer, as they simply didn't know. The British interrogators vainly kept up their onslaught trying to determine what they were dealing with – perhaps it was a new gun or a bomb? Perhaps an aircraft or radar system?

The prisoners were as baffled as their captors; they had no idea what the British were talking about. The campaign lasted for several days and then, as abruptly as it began, the interrogators simply dropped the question and never referred to it again.

U-boat Crisis

The U-boat posed the greatest threat to merchant vessels during the conflict. It has been argued that it was the most significant risk to Britain's survival of the war. Attacking convoys from the cover of the waves, the U-boats were understandably feared by ships' crews and any information or device that could enable the British to better find and destroy the German subs was treated like gold dust.

The U-boats preferred to loiter around the Atlantic, picking off supply ships in night attacks. They were to remain a significant threat until Germany surrendered, causing the Battle of the Atlantic and the constant need to defend against prowling U-boats. In the early days of the war, Allied supply ships were sitting ducks for the Germans, who sank as many as they could with little resistance. The enemy navy crews referred to this period as 'The Happy Time', as striking the helpless convoys was so easy.

The Atlantic was Britain's lifeline; troops, food and military supplies all came across that stretch of ocean. Hitler was well aware that if he could conquer the Atlantic and turn it into Nazi-controlled territory by the terror of his U-boats, then Britain had little chance of outlasting the war. Without the Atlantic convoys, Britain would either be starved into submission or its army would become so under-equipped, due to reduced manpower or weapons, that Germany could simply overwhelm them. A similar tactic in the First World War had almost crippled Great Britain.

Despite this, both countries were arguably under-prepared for ocean combat when war broke out. Germany only had forty-six operational vessels and these were largely surface vessels, as opposed to submarines. However, on 3 September 1939, as war was officially declared, a German U-boat torpedoed the British liner *Athenia*, and thus Hitler made his intentions clear.

Britain fought back by developing new systems for spotting the U-boats; the earliest of these was the ASDIC system, a primitive type of sonar that the Royal Navy relied heavily on. The surface vessels posed less of a threat, and the British found them relatively easy to pick off – important triumphs including the sinking of the *Graf Spee* and the *Bismarck*. U-boats were a trickier problem, and with the conquest of France and Norway bases for these German subs could be moved forward, enabling the crafts to travel further afield and be supplied with air support from the Focke-Wulf FW200.

Britain was desperately short of escort vessels to protect its convoys, and with the U–boat threat suddenly closer to home they had had to move shipping routes away from vulnerable ports. The Royal Navy provided protection along certain stretches of the Atlantic, but everyone knew it was not enough. President Roosevelt went some way to easing the problem by supplying fifty old American destroyers to Britain, in exchange for bases in the British territory of the West Indies.

Even so, as Dr Gary Sheffield writing for BBC History states, 'U–boats, supplemented by mines, aircraft and surface ships, succeeded in sinking three million tons of Allied shipping between the fall of France in June 1940 and the end of the year.'[1]

The German subs were already counteracting the effects of the ASDIC system that the Royal Navy relied on so much, by patrolling in groups termed Wolf Packs. They would surface only at night to launch attacks, making them nearly impossible to detect in time.

Britain introduced a number of tactics to survive this period, including supplying defensive vessels and aircraft to cover the convoys. But these were only scratching the surface; to produce a truly effective defence, interviewing as many U–boat crew as they could get their hands on was vital. This in itself was not easy as U–boats, when destroyed, often took their entire crew with them – a lucky man was a U–boat crewman who survived to be captured.

Despite the difficulties, the first official POWs in British hands were from a U–boat. The nature of the questions the interrogators asked these men is indicative of the monumental lack of knowledge Britain was suffering from at the time concerning the German subs:

Interrogation of two members of the crew of 'U.35' on 16 January 1940.
[Concerning patrol routes]
During the days immediately preceding the sinking of U.35 she had been on patrol between the Scottish and Norwegian coasts. The weather was particularly bad, and it was stated that boats prefer to submerge to a depth of 30 metres (98ft) rather than remain on the surface.
[Asking confirmation of the belief that U–boats used smoke signals when underwater]
It was definitely stated that U–boats are not fitted with a gun for firing smoke signals when submerged.

[Wanting to determine the route U-boats would take to reach the Atlantic]

The prisoners examined denied emphatically that any attempt would be made to pass through the Straits of Dover if it was intended to operate in the Atlantic. They said that they pass as far North as possible.

[Trying to ascertain where the U-boats were based]

No definite confirmation was obtained regarding the position where U-boats lie in Wilhelmshaven. It was stated that they would be berthed where there was space available.

[Regarding signals to German planes]

U-boats have no special recognition signals for communicating with aircraft. On sighting aircraft they submerge at once without waiting to establish the identity of the machine.[2]

Just from this rather flimsy report it is obvious that the British were virtually in the dark when it came to these marauding vessels that were doing such a fine job of sinking merchant ships. The Atlantic had become a Nazi playground, unsafe for civilian vessels. The Germans were well aware of their superiority in the seas, even when it was to their detriment. When an early party of POWs were to be shipped from Britain to Canada there was almost a riot, as the men, mostly U-boat crew, knew their comrades would be lurking in the waters ready to sink the merchant vessels. They were sent anyway, and one vessel was attacked and sunk with loss of life by a stalking U-boat.

Britain needed to catch up fast. It was no use relying on half-reports and rumours about underwater smoke signals or U-boat bases; they needed concrete facts and they needed them fast. The early documents of the various interrogation files held in The National Archives are almost exclusively concerned with U-boat systems and tactics, showing the phenomenal power these machines had and the pressure they put on the British. Churchill would later remark '… the only thing that ever really frightened me during the war was the U-boat peril.'

Another interrogation of three prisoners in September of 1940 shows that the interrogators were beginning to refine their questions and understand their subject better. The men were from U-boats U51 and U52:

Kommos is straightforward, reliable and discreet and will not disclose what he considers to be secret e.g. he refused to say what was his home town and which ship he came from. He is 24, has been a seaman for 4 years, prior to that was a member of the Hitler youth movement ... Telegraphist in the U52 in which he had been for 2 years. He had been in another U-boat previously, for a short time.

The U52 was not modern, it has an ordinary sender–receiver communication set and M/F D/F equipment, which was accurate to within about 40.

Under water communications was by hydrophone.

Ciphering was done by him or an officer.

W/T [wireless telegraphy] silence was only broke by request of control, and weather reports were added to such reports. Signals were sometimes made even from the Atlantic.

He knows what I.I.s mean, but said he would not divulge the meaning, though I judged when I put it to him that he did not deny that I.I.s represented weather reports.[3]

Irich Lange from Berlin is 21 years old, has been a seaman for 2 years and was a leading telegraphist on the U52. He is frank and reliable.

Ciphering was sometimes done by F.O. Telegraphist Kommos or himself, and sometimes by an officer.

Signals were never made except at the request of the control station. Signals contained general information and sometimes weather reports and statements of position. Weather reports were sometimes given alone, but whether alone or with other signals, they were indicated by I.I.s, and contained 5 groups.

Neither weather reports nor other signals were necessarily made at the same time each day.

Seaman Fathois from U51 is 33 and comes from Vienna. He is ... unreliable and ignorant. He regards himself as a German rather than as an Austrian and was like his father, a social democrat before the Anschluss. He was [a] button turner by profession, but was unemployed at the beginning of 1939, when he was sent to Germany as a labour conscript.

At the end of his course in November 1939, he had no special interest in any branch of seamanship, so was drafted to the U-boat school at Wilhelmshaven, from where he joined the U51 in March 1940.

His jobs were those of an ordinary seaman, but he professes knowledge of the jobs of other members of the crew, which he claims to have acquired through general conversation on board.

He stated that the U51 was entirely refitted after her first sinking, but that there were no new features among the fittings.

Once again the interrogators were using their skills to unravel stories and play people against each other. It didn't matter that Kommos chose to be discreet and not discuss 'I.I.' signals; his comrade Lange would prove more talkative. The same applied in all situations, when interviewing a number of men on the same subject it was highly unlikely that they would all refuse to talk, indeed certain members, like the cocky Fathois, would be only too keen to shed light as a way of boosting their own appearance in front of the British.

By now Britain was beginning to see light at the end of the tunnel when it came to U-boats; it had taken months of extensive interviews and intelligence gathering, but the German subs were gradually becoming less of a mystery.

When it came to the interrogation of Ernst Felbeck, a 26-year-old telegraphist on the *U13*, it is obvious the British interrogators were now far more up to speed on their U-boats. There was no more discussion of rumoured underwater smoke signals, but the interrogators were clearly focusing on communications – the last vital piece of the puzzle. If they could intercept and understand the messages the U-boats were sending, the advantages would be tremendous and could save thousands of lives. Anyone involved with telegraphy or ciphering on a submarine, therefore, became of instant importance.

'Felbeck is intelligent, straightforward and fairly communicative and states that a subject is secret when he does not intend to answer a question. When forced by pressing to give an evasive answer he shows obvious embarrassment. He … was a typesetter before joining the navy in 1933, trained at Stralsund and took his signal course at Flensburg from April to October 1934 when he acquired great interest in the theory and practice of W/T.'[4]

Felbeck's case report began with the usual assessment of character that the interrogators knew was so vital. The case officers had to make quick decisions on a man's temperament to enable the intelligence officers who received the information to decide whether to believe it and whether it required cross referencing. On a subject as vital to the war effort as U-boats, this was particularly important and there was no room for error. Fortunately, Felbeck's own reticence made the information he did impart (however grudgingly) more convincing to the interrogators.

As a telegraphist, Felbeck was closely interviewed on the wireless communications aboard the U-boats. By this point the British were also no longer in the dark about submarine bases and knew that Wilhelmshaven was a primary one.

'[Wireless telegraphy] Communication was with Wilhelmshaven on the four voyages [Felbeck] made in U13 in the North Sea after he joined her in 1940. The set was permanently tuned in harbour at the beginning of each voyage. The tuning dials were scaled in degrees and only the captain had access to the calibration curves. On two of the voyages U13 was tuned to a different frequency from that used on the other two. (Note) Felbeck was pressed about frequencies and the last sentence may be untrue.'

The interrogators were also keen to discover how effective their own navy's tactics against the U-boats were, and how good their ability to detect U-boats was. In this instance the only way to learn the truth was to have a witness from an attack. It was an ironic situation as the interrogators had to hope that any Royal Navy attack on a U-boat was not serious enough to completely destroy the vessel and thus make survival of the crew unlikely. Felbeck was one of those lucky survivors.

'Felbeck took a special course in submarine detection in December 1939. The German system is superior to, though based on, a similar principle to the British. When asked what system he supposed was used by the H.M. [Royal Navy] he replied that he knew it was not based on sound wave reflection, because although U13 had been chased and depth charged on more than one occasion, only once had a high pitched intermittent note been generally audible in the boat.'

Felbeck's interview revealed there were still gaps in the navy's ability to protect convoys from the German Wolf Packs. It could have been disheartening to hear of the British failings, but it was necessary if progress was to be made to improve defences. In this way the interrogator was one of the most vital personnel of the war; they were the only ones who could unlock the full mysteries behind the inner workings of U-boat craft and crew.

The Battle of the Atlantic raged throughout the war years with ups and downs for both sides. Britain's constant supply issues, and frantic attempts to build new merchant vessels to replace those that had been sunk, would be compensated by the improved ability of the navy to detect and sink U-boats, the addition of aircraft to protect the convoys and the significant breakthroughs of intelligence in the capturing and decrypting of the Enigma machine (see below). If ever there was a situation where the interrogators had to work tirelessly to keep up to speed with the latest German military developments, this was it. The Germans were not fools; they constantly adapted to counteract British successes, meanwhile the Royal Navy was always playing catch up. In the end, however, the British found themselves the aggressors, destroying forty-five U-boats between April and May 1943. This was the turning point. Hitler recognised his losses were outranking his gains and he withdrew his ships, maintaining a significantly diminished presence in the Atlantic (though the British knew the threat to convoys was still high).

Intelligence, via captured U-boats and the interrogation of their crews, had played an indispensable role in this triumph. The risks could not have been higher as the war casualty figures demonstrate: between 75,000 and 85,000 Allied seaman were killed in the Atlantic. Around 28,000 – out of a total of 41,000 – U-boat crewmen were killed, two-thirds of whom died in the Battle of the Atlantic, proving just how difficult it was to capture a U-boat telegraphist alive for questioning. The loss of life was horrendous, but it could have been so much worse. Simply put, if Britain had lost the Battle of the Atlantic then they would have lost the war. For the interrogators, this would become one of the key events that would prove their worth and have an immediate, direct impact on the fate of Great Britain.

An Enigma

In 1918 Arthur Scherbius, a German inventor, filed a patent for an overgrown typewriter that was the basis for the most dangerous mechanical encryption machine of the war. The Enigma machine, as it came to be known, was the most advanced device of its type ever manufactured, capable of billions of combinations that made cracking its coded messages seem almost impossible.

The Enigma machine was commercially available during the 1920s, but the Nazis were quick to pick up on its potential outside of the domestic realm. By 1928 the machine was serving as the primary encryption device of the German military and during the war they would purchase over 30,000 machines, believing completely in its inability to be cracked.

The design of the Enigma machine was intrinsically complicated. The main components were three rotors (they looked like discs) that implemented complex substitutions of letters for coding. The rotors were divided into twenty-six segments with randomly connected electrical contacts on the front and back. These rotors defined the nature of the substitution that would encrypt a message. When a key on the typewriter of the machine was pressed an electrical current passed into the rotor and then to a bulb that lit up to indicate a certain letter.

It is after this point that the process takes on an extra level of complication. The first rotor, after the key has been struck, moves on one place so that the code permutation changes. The first letter of the message is therefore in a different code to the second letter, and then to the third letter and so on. After each letter the code changes. When the first rotor has moved through its cycle of twenty-six divisions, the second rotor then moves one place, changing the permutations for the next twenty-six letters completely. The third rotor only moves when the second rotor has completed its own cycle of twenty-six turns.

To make things even trickier, the rotors could be arranged in any order (so, for instance, if they were numbered 1, 2, 3, they could be arranged 2, 3, 1 or 3, 1, 2) and in the latter years of the war there was a choice of five different rotors. There was also a plugboard, like an old-fashioned telephone exchange, which enabled two numbers to be switched before they even entered the rotors, again in later models up to thirteen plug interchanges could be used, though it was usually only ten. If that wasn't enough, there was a ring that attached to a rotor and determined when in that rotor's cycle the next disc changed (after twenty-five turns instead of twenty-six, for instance).[5]

In many cases the machine was more complicated than its operators could cope with, and the German military created standard daily lists of machine configurations for their telegraphists to follow. As in so many cases, it was the human element of the procedure that let the system down.

Prior to the war it became clear that the Enigma machine could prove a dangerous strategic 'weapon' in the hands of the Germans and efforts were made to begin to crack it. Polish cryptologist Marian Rejewski was the one who recognised the threat. He was able to obtain design specifications for an early form of the Enigma. This design only used three rotors and six plugboards, making it simpler to decode. He was unwittingly assisted by the military habit of sending a repeated message of the three-letter rotor key to be used that day for the benefit of German receiving operators. This minor slip-up enabled Rejewski to design a machine for decoding the messages. This was called the '*Bomba*' or, when it arrived in England, the 'Bombe'.

Poland was happy to share this information with Britain and France, and the Bombe, along with information on the early Enigma machine, arrived at Bletchley Park where it would spend the rest of the war being used to intercept German messages.

There was actually a very simple way of breaking an Enigma code. If you knew the set-up of the original machine that sent the message, you could configure another machine in the same way and type the message back in for it to be automatically unscrambled. But this required knowledge of the daily set-up plans of the Germans. Even the Bombe needed to be set up to suit the Enigma machine the encoded message was written on. Everything became more complicated in 1938 when the Germans altered their Enigma system, thwarting the Polish attempt to decrypt it and leaving the British, once again, out of date.

Now British mathematicians Alan Turing and Gordon Welchman took up the gauntlet. Realising that German encrypted messages often contained the same words or phrases, such as a general's name or a weather report, they began to be able to guess short parts of messages. They also knew that a letter could not be encrypted as itself (i.e. X could not be coded as X to fool code-crackers); this made their task slightly easier. Using these nuggets of information they were able to make educated guesses or 'cribs' that could then be used to configure the Bombe for decoding.

It was at this point the interrogators became important. The more information Turing and Welchman had on the way the Germans used their Enigma machines, any specific codes they sent to indicate certain reports, or on the daily set-up instructions, could enable them to crack codes faster. It would also help them to determine which messages should be decrypted first, as the amount of communications traffic being intercepted was overwhelming and priority needed to be given to anything about immediate military manoeuvres (weather reports could wait).

Finding suitable candidates for providing information on the Enigma was not always easy. Officers were usually in charge of setting the rotors, rather than the ordinary telegraphists and operators; these were men who knew the value of keeping their mouths shut. Prompting answers from anyone involved in Enigma operation could be tricky without subterfuge.

When Funkmaat May (Radioman Third Class) came into British hands in January 1940 it was immediately recognised that he could hold vital information, but he was cagey and reluctant to talk. Initial interviews managed to whittle small chunks of information from him, such as that 'E' at the start of a transmission indicated an Enigma message was coming (with usual German bluntness). He also explained that in the preamble of the message there would be a number that referred to a table.

'Thus if 752 is transmitted in a preamble before the message it indicates three letters (say LMJ) and the Walzen are revolved by hand until the letters appear in the windows on top and ciphering in the ordinary way is then done.'[6]

This was a highly significant slice of information for the British, who could pass such information to Turing and Welchman for quicker decryption. It might seem odd that Funkmaat May would reveal such a key way of operating the Enigma machine, when on other aspects, such as wireless frequencies, he was reluctant to say anything. But in fact it was due to a ploy the interrogators chose to use with him – the chatty, 'you don't need to tell me, I know already' trick.

'In reading this report it should be remembered that Lieut. Pennell [the interrogator] adopts the attitude that our own S/M service uses an Enigma machine, and as he is very "friendly" with the prisoner, they compare details.'

It was as simple as that. The men were just having a 'chat' about something they both knew about. Funkmaat May was unfortunate not to have been briefed that the British did not possess such technology on their vessels, and as his little conversations carried on with Pennell he became more and more confident about talking. After all, if they already had Enigma machines, what harm could it do?

May was very helpful, explaining how the wheels of the machine were changed roughly every two days by an officer, even going as far as to say it took about sixty seconds to make the change. He also provided a series of helpful diagrams including the following:

> The 'Stechens' [plugboards] ... These, he said, are roughly changed 1–2 a day (before he had said about 3 times) by the funkmaat. The layout of the 'stechen' is given below:

1	2	3	4	5	6	7	8
o	o	o	o	o	o	o	o
o	o	o	o	o	o	o	o

9	10	11	12	13	14	15	16
o	o	o	o	o	o	o	o
o	o	o	o	o	o	o	o

(N.B. They may be lettered, not numbered)

17	18	19	20	21	22	23	24
o	o	o	o	o	o	o	o
o	o	o	o	o	o	o	o

> It can be seen the holes are double and the connector must be made with double plugs similar to electric light plugs, there is apparently only one lead between them.

May's helpfulness was increased by Pennell's quiet comparisons to the 'British Engima', which encouraged a natural Aryan pride to stir in the funkmaat:

> I remarked to May that our Enigma machine functioned very slowly and was unsuitable for urgent operational signals and consequently we used a table. He said that their Enigma was as quick as anything. May then drew out a piece of paper showing their method of working, it is divided into 8 columns, e.g.:

> | D/L | | CODED | | | | | |
> |---|---|---|---|---|---|---|---|
> | Z | W | E | I | G | J | P | L |
> | Z | E | R | S | N | L | F | C |
> | T | O | R | E | D | D | N | I |
> | R | S | K | V | L | V | S | T |

The funkmaat presses Z on the key and when Q lights up his opposite number writes it down in the corresponding column.

Funkmaat May was not the first or last to be fooled by such a game. Pennell built up a fabricated friendship with him so that the interrogation became more of a cosy chat. They could have been old comrades meeting in a cafe to discuss news. Such a ploy broke down the barriers of enemies and, by playing on German national pride, Pennell soon had his victim happily gossiping about Nazi technological superiority.

There is no doubt that such interrogations were fundamental to helping break the Enigma code. They provided the human element that was necessary to work out the foibles of the system, and at the end of the day it was this human element that also let down Enigma. It was the need to let everyone know the code, the need to keep daily lists and, ultimately, it was the need to employ thousands of young men to operate the devices, men who, under the right circumstances, would forget to hold their tongues.

Breaking the Enigma was a combined effort of Polish ingenuity, British mathematics and German gullibility before the interrogators. Once again, the interview rooms of places such as CSDIC camps and the London Cage helped to unravel a wartime mystery and save lives. That they did so through misdirection and lies does not diminish their triumph.

Taunting the Tigers

In June 1942 a raging battle of words began in *The Times* about Britain's failure to produce tanks that could compete with the German armaments.

'We were told after the summer's fighting of 1941 that German prisoners in North Africa had commented on the excellence of our tanks, but marvelled that we armed them with "pop-guns".' Wrote Mr Sidney Clive, '… the armament of our tanks in Libya … seem to show that the Germans in that theatre are still in advance of us as regards that armament, what a reflection upon our foresight, our methods and our organisation. Rommel, after experience of a summer's fighting in the desert, says he must have refrigerator tanks. By the following summer he gets them. It is inevitable that one should ask oneself whether or not our commanders displayed similar foresight.'[7]

Scathing enough, but even more voices added to the backlash against the British tank. A Mr Milholland, veteran artillery officer of the First World War, wrote a critical letter of the 75mm guns mounted onto British tanks:

'I should say that this gun would be practically useless for accurate shooting at either moving or stationary objects, because fine adjustments could not be made accurately or quickly by moving a 28 ton mass, and the shock of discharge would make it necessary to relay after each round by the same clumsy method. It would have no real chance against its opposite number, the German Mk IV tank, which has as its main armament a 75mm gun, electrically fired in a rotating cupola, or against the German self-propelled field guns mounted on tank chassis of which they have both 3in and 6in, according to the wireless and newspapers. Possibly the new 88mm long-range guns are also mounted in the same way.'[8]

The 88mm guns were part of the newly designed Tiger tanks, the next step in German armoured vehicles designed to counter the unexpectedly formidable armour of the Soviet army. Compared to this, Britain's tanks looked like ineffectual toys – the mounted 'pop-guns' as the Germans laughingly referred to them. Worse was to come as the Germans began to mass their tanks for an offensive against Russia in July of that year.

'The German preparations suggest that German tank columns are nearly ready to attempt almost immediately two new thrusts [against Russia].'[9]

With all this worrying information it was once again the role of the interrogators to find out as much as they could about this new danger – the German Tiger tank.

The Tiger I (officially the Panzerkampfwagen Tiger Ausf. E) was developed in 1942 in answer to the heavy tanks the Russians were successfully deploying against the Germans. Formidable and feared by nearly all opponents, the Tiger was quickly the subject of choice in POW interrogations, but finding reliable men who could give intelligence on this new super-weapon was once again a problem. The British had to rely on whatever sources they could get their hands on, such as Obergefreiter Kurt Bachmann who had seen a Tiger tank in a workshop in Tunis.

Bachmann could outline basics of the tank structure, roughly calculating that the vehicle was 8m long and 4m wide, but he was frustratingly vague, unable to say where the superstructure was divided from the suspension, and in half a mind that the tank had some sort of skirting armour.

Despite his failings, Bachmann had actually clambered into a tank while it was being built and could give vital information on the early workings of the turret and bulkheads. The interrogators took extensive notes of everything he said, hoping that it would prove vital to the war effort. Even so, they were aware of the limitations of their prisoner and took his more staggering claims with a pinch of salt.

'P/W alleges that there are six machine guns (!) in this tank.'[10] It actually had two Maschinengewehr 34s (German machine guns). 'P/W claims to have heard that the armour thickness of the front plate is 35cm (!).' The frontal hull armour was in reality only 100mm or 10cm, a full 25cm short of Buchmann's statement, though it is feasible that he had been listening to exaggeration for propaganda purposes – it would not have been the first time the Germans had misled their own men to serve their own purposes.

Yet Bachmann had even more fantastical claims: 'P/W states, and the dimensions given confirm, that the gun has to be loaded from below. P/W does not remember seeing any hoisting or ramming gear, and talks of loading by hand at the rate of 24 rounds a minute (!).' No wonder the interrogators were sceptical, the shells for the gun weighed several kilos (the Tiger II's shells ranged in weight from 7.5kg to just over 10kg) and Bachmann was suggesting they could be repeatedly loaded in under three seconds!

There was one area, however, where Bachmann's knowledge could be significant. He had witnessed the damage caused by a British anti-tank gun.

'The tank had, according to P/W, been hit at short range by a British shell allegedly from a 12cm (60 pounder) gun. He states he observed the hole, or rather the dent, closely, and had made from memory a plasticine model which has been passed to MI.10. The dimensions of the hole are stated by him to have been 12cm … The small ridges of rolled petalling which appear inside the hole were much more sharp edged than P/W could make them with this material.'

Why was Bachmann such a helpful subject? That has to remain between him and his interrogators, though it seems they had their own concerns about his co-operative nature judging by the numbers of 'alleges' and 'according tos' used in the report. When Bachmann had been so woefully wrong about armour and ammunitions, it was not surprising his testimony on the damage (or lack of) done by a British gun to a Tiger was seen as suspect. No doubt the interrogators hoped that he had been mistaken, either in the amount of damage or the size of the weapon used.

From 1942 onwards the Allies were deeply concerned about the super-tanks Germany was producing, with constantly updated and new designs.

It wasn't just their armaments that made them pause for breath: it was how the tanks were used. In 1945 the Americans were having their own Sherman tanks criticised in the popular press, while the Tiger IIs were causing heavy casualties.

Life magazine reported: 'The Russians and Germans are agreed that [tanks] should be sent not only against infantry positions but also against artillery, anti-tank guns and other tanks. The Americans and British try to avoid tank battles. They use self-propelled guns against enemy guns and tanks, and call on nimble little tanks to clean out infantry positions. Nevertheless, in battle American tanks run into enemy guns and tanks to their great discomfiture.'[11]

Critics were only too eager to point out the Allied tanks' failings against the seemingly unstoppable Tigers: '… American tankmen have long complained of at least eight superiorities of the enemy tanks; 1) low silhouette which makes it harder to hit 2) wider tracks which give better flotation 3) superior gun 4) uncluttered, more comfortable interior [no doubt American generals took great note of this particular superiority!] 5) superior vision slits 6) thicker and better angled frontal plate 7) a track-locking device that enables the German tank to spin round on one track 8) superior storage space for ammunition.'[12]

In the face of such damning comparisons the Tiger tank should have been the ultimate of armoured vehicles, but the interrogators through their work – that then fed into the various intelligence systems and ultimately to the commanders on the front – knew differently.

The Tiger tank, amazing as it sounded, was supremely over-engineered. It used expensive and labour-intensive materials and production was lengthy and costly. Those superior tracks, with their locking devices, were prone to breaking down and leaving the tank immobile, and though generally reliable the Tiger proved difficult to transport due to its interlocking wheels. The Germans made less than 1,500 of their wonder machines (between August 1942 and August 1944) and this was the Allies' reprieve.

By 1943 *The Times* could report 'TANKS ATTACKED IN A PASS, MANY IN FLAMES … The enemy was powerfully attacked by United States Aircraft, and in one sweep 12 tanks were set on fire.'[13] Contrary to Bachmann's report that 60-pounder guns had merely dented a tank's hull, the same paper could report that '[In Tunisia] The tanks came under the accurate fire of our 25 pounders concealed in a small wood … and eighteen were destroyed.'[14] A photograph accompanying the article showed a burnt-out tank, the turret and its cupola virtually gone, and that fearsomely thick hull smashed and crumpled in on itself.

The story of the Tiger tank and the interrogators is difficult to assess as either a success or failure. In certain quarters of public opinion it would seem the latter, on the other hand, Britain was successfully repelling tank attacks; just how much of that was the direct result of prisoner interrogations is open to debate. Like the U-boat crewmen, just getting hold of someone from a panzer division could be tricky. Tanks notoriously consumed their crews when destroyed; direct hits could be devastating, wounding or killing men. Managing to apprehend survivors from such devastation was a seemingly impossible task. Panzer crews had a higher kill-to-losses ratio than the rest of the German army, and in the final year of the war it was as much as five times higher.

On this case the interrogators fell between the lines; they found some useful information, but they also had to battle against half-truths, rumours and lies. They neither had the triumphant success of the Enigma, nor the depressing failure of the cases that are to follow, but the Tiger proved that not all of Germany's war secrets would give themselves up to the calculating minds of the British interrogators.

When Death Meant More than Life

Failure could come in many forms for the interrogators. At one extreme, it was the disappointment of not apprehending a target. Such an example was that of Dutch agent Englebertus Fukken, alias William Ter Braak, who parachuted into England in the winter of 1940 and managed to stay at large for six months until April 1941 when, short on money and ideas, he hid in an air-raid shelter and shot himself with his Abwehr-issued pistol. Suicide, in fact, was not only the interrogators' biggest fear but, to them, a sign of failure to either get a man to talk or to recognise that he was a risk to himself. The ultimate interrogation failures could be argued to be Hitler and those of his lackeys, who killed themselves rather than fall into British hands. Right up until the end of the war Britain expected to interrogate her arch-enemies; Himmler was in fact in British custody when he committed suicide during a strip search.

A dead man is of no use to an interrogator, nor is, of course, the wrong man. And the British were not exempt from making errors and suspecting the wrong suspect. In a climate of war, where interrogators are faced with a continual parade of foreign individuals, each trying to convince of their innocence, the odds of someone who was truly innocent being caught up in the chaos were, not surprisingly, high. No stone, metaphorically, could remain unturned, so the slightest hint of suspicion about a person raised alarm bells in the cynical minds of the authorities.

It was an instance of misguided honour that led Claude de la Fere into such a situation. He was French and had fled his homeland for England in a canoe. If that wasn't enough to raise the eyebrows of his interrogators, though completely true, it was his efforts to conceal the nature of his birth that had them chewing their pens and thinking the worst.

De la Fere was born out of wedlock. To the honourable-minded refugee it was the greatest of sins and he desperately tried to hide it from his inter-rogators. To do so his lies became more and more elaborate and this had the hardened authorities reading sinister motives into his arrival. He was dispatched to Camp 020, the repository for suspected enemy agents, and there spent four months clinging to his lies about his origins. It was a par-ticularly foolish game in the wartime climate, especially as enemy spies were routinely executed. De la Fere's motives were simply that of shame and embarrassment. Finally, after intensive interrogation, he broke and confessed to his illegitimate birth.

Stunned, and no doubt mildly disappointed that this was the only revela-tion the French canoeist had to give, the authorities of Camp 020 released him. The commandant noted in his report, 'de la Fere is a sensitive bastard who crossed the Channel in a canoe …'

De la Fere walked free in England and became a BBC announcer.

A more disturbing case that casts a pall over our interrogators was that of Hendrik van Dam. Van Dam was working for the Belgian Mission to Seamen in London when an informant for Camp 020, previously known for providing reliable information, denounced him to his superiors. The story told to the authorities was that some months earlier van Dam had been in contact with an officer of the German intelligence service while in

Paris. That nugget of information was enough to have van Dam escorted to Camp 020's headquarters in Ham.

Van Dam was a sensitive character who, under the pressure of interrogation, began to suffer mentally. The usual camp tactics of psychologically undermining a traitor had a more sinister effect on the innocent Hendrik. For four months he protested his innocence and was thrown into despair by the cold disbelief of his interrogators.

Van Dam broke, but not in a way the camp wanted or liked. He began to hallucinate, and there seems no reason to believe that his nightmares were anything but genuine. The power of mental manipulation was known to the 020 interrogators; with their special trick of Cell Fourteen and other psychological pressures. On van Dam these mind games had a disastrous effect and he told Huysmans, the stool pigeon mentioned earlier, that he could hear the agonised screams of a woman being tortured in a neighbouring cell.

To another prisoner, Peereboom, he spoke of the noises he heard in the night caused by ghosts and spirits, which were especially loud on Thursday nights and kept him awake with their crashes from above. In fact Thursday night was guest night in the officers' mess, so the ghouls van Dam heard were nothing more than heavy-footed visitors. But van Dam was deteriorating, and laughing off his Thursday night ghosts could not change that. When he started to hear the bells of Hell ringing for him and actually welcomed them, the camp authorities decided to call it a day.

They released Hendrik van Dam as a free and innocent man and sent him on his way, with only relief that they were excused from his madness. Their concern was only for the safety of Britain and her citizens; what became of the hallucinating van Dam after he left their care was none of their business.

Camp 020 at Ham had a good reputation for breaking prisoners with minimal pressure. A combination of tiring interrogations and evidence from decrypted messages was usually enough to break most agents. This was not surprising, considering many were the products of German blackmail or financial greed; many agents had little or no loyalty to their masters. Some, however, showed dogged determination to withhold the truth even when reminded of the death penalty they faced. No amount of psychological pressure could sway them, and though only a handful failed to fall before the 020 interrogators' might, they were significant in the way they tenaciously refused to confess.

Frustrating and time-consuming was the case of Lambertus Elferink. A Dutch-born journalist, Elferink, it was hoped, would prove to be a font of knowledge on German espionage activity in South Africa. South Africa was a bubbling pot of spy activity for the Germans throughout the war and many of their agents found themselves there. Elferink was sent there in 1940 and, like many Axis agents, he would have been expected to spread the Nazi ideal, ferment dissent in the dominion and shake the foundations of the Imperial war effort. Nazism was a growing trend in the region and the hub for spies was Lourenco Marques, colonial capital of Portuguese East Africa (now Mozambique). With the population in South Africa, and even members of the Cabinet, supportive of the Axis powers, Elferink could have freely promoted Nazism with open and obvious propaganda.

Britain was understandably anxious about this hotbed of German activity and launched many counter-espionage initiatives. Large amounts of resources and energy were piled into uncovering the activities of the German espionage teams, among which was the use of ISOS.

Oliver Strachey had actually left the ISOS department in 1942 to go to Canada, but even after his replacement, Denys Page, had his feet firmly under his desk, the old code name for decrypts stuck.

It was during 1942, while Denys Page was still settling into his new role, that ISOS intercepted messages discussing a German agent code-named 'Hamlet'. The agent was extremely active and in receipt of large sums of money from his masters. It didn't take them long to confirm that 'Hamlet' was Elferink and for almost two years they monitored his movements and activities. At the end of 1943 it was decided Elferink's run of freedom should be swiftly curtailed; the interrogators wanted him in their clutches revealing his secrets. So arrangements were organised for Elferink to be conscripted into the Dutch army and sent to England. He would be arrested immediately on landing.

Elferink found himself swept away from his life of luxury and peace in South Africa to the grey shores of England, believing he was destined to fight against his masters, only to be arrested and escorted to Ham as soon as his boots hit British soil.

Elferink faced his interrogators with a steady gaze and pretence of innocence. Young, blonde and slightly tanned from the African sun, he acted in complete ignorance of why he had been detained. He had only just arrived, after all, to serve Britain via the Dutch army.

The interrogators were faced with an impenetrable wall of feigned confusion and astonishment. The only evidence they had against the young man were the ISOS messages and these they preferred to use only sparingly, less their captives learn about the system and potentially report back. So, as Elferink faced his interrogator, both men were holding back vital information; one to save his skin, the other to save his country.

At the first interrogation both parties were skirting each other. The interrogator made much play of using Hamlet quotes and taunts to shake Elferink. Elferink maintained his mask of bemused innocence, neither responding to harshness nor politeness; he offered nothing about his espionage activities, finding the whole idea mildly amusing. The interrogator tried to breakthrough via another tactic, pointing out the oddities of Elferink's finances while in South Africa, but he still could not get a response and the first interview ended in frustration for Camp 020.

To have a spy with potential gold information sitting in a cell and refusing to speak was exasperating for the 020 team. In situations like this sometimes ISOS's reliability would be questioned; misinterpretation or misunderstanding of a message could have led the interrogators astray. But on this occasion they were certain the information was accurate. Elferink was a German spy, nothing could be clearer, his activities had been monitored since 1942, his finances were heavily supplemented by the Nazis, and yet he would not talk.

Months of interrogation went by, but even when new information that could be openly used from captured German agents was presented to him, Elferink kept silent. The interrogators discovered that there were some men, rare but nonetheless there, that could not be broken. Hours and hours of interviews hardened Elferink and his casual silence became even stronger. He didn't slip and he never acknowledged the evidence presented to him. In the end it was Britain that had to concede defeat, and in July 1945 Elferink, still acting baffled at his confinement and interrogation, was sent to Holland as one of the few to defy British intelligence.

Notes
1 Dr Gary Sheffield, 'The Battle of the Atlantic: The U-boat Peril', BBC History *www.bbc.co.uk/history/worldwars/wwtwo/battle_atlantic_01.shtml*.
2 PRO records.
3 PRO records.
4 PRO records.

5 For further explanations of the workings of an Enigma machine refer to: David G. Luenberger, *Information Science*, Princeton University Press, 2008.

6 PRO records.

7 'Tanks and Guns, Rival Armaments in Libya, The German Lead', in *The Times*, Saturday, 27 June 1942.

8 'Tanks and Guns, German and British Design, Power of Manoeuvre', in *The Times*, Monday, 29 June 1942.

9 'German Tanks Mass, Preparations for a New Drive', in *The Times*, Tuesday, 28 July 1942.

10 PRO records, grammatical notations are those of the interrogators.

11 'The Battle of the Tanks', *Life*, 26 March 1945.

12 Ibid.

13 'Attack by German Tanks in Tunisia', in *The Times*, Monday, 1 February 1943.

14 'German Tanks Beaten Off', in *The Times*, Saturday, 6 February 1943.

7

THE LONDON CAGE

Queuing for rations outside the shops on Kensington High Street, the busy wartime shopper would have barely spared a glance for the ornate gates and tree-lined avenue that led to one of the most exclusive areas of London. Down that avenue, where grand carriages and polished black cars glided, escorting the wealthiest members of society, lay the Palace Gardens, the grandest of addresses. Foreign princes had their London dwellings in the carefully tended grounds, and London's elite stared out of towering Georgian windows into a world where every neighbour was a millionaire several times over.

The average 1940s Londoner knew nothing of this mysterious world of luxury and expense right on their doorstep. If they did, by chance, stop to catch a glimpse of the Georgian façades, elegant in their classical style, it probably would not have occured to them that the last black car that drove down the avenue was not carrying a millionaire or an aristocrat, but a German prisoner heading for the most feared British interrogation centre. Unless, that is, they had heard the rumours that a place called the London Cage was housed in the magnificent gardens, and that it was used as a sorting centre to organise prisoners into camps.

Early mornings indeed saw tired, worn-looking men in enemy uniforms bustled down the tree-lined avenue prior to being sent elsewhere in the country. For ordinary German soldiers travelling down the grand avenue and looking at the glory of British architecture, it would have been an awesome and daunting sight. The British, Hitler had screamed at them, would be destroyed because they were ignorant, old-fashioned and weak, yet here they were displaying the country's capital glory to mere prisoners. If this was where they held prisoners before assigning camps, the prisoners thought, what must the rest of the country be like?

Cars pulled up before houses 6, 7 and 8, allowing the magnificence of the surroundings to dawn on the enemy. These men, who had spent months in ditches and dug-outs, fighting lice and disease while trying to make a dent in the Allies, could now see Britain at her best: the towering edifices, the manicured grounds and houses glistening with wealth, and just outside the gates ordinary British civilians were going about their day. Britain no longer seemed quite the backward, weak little island Nazi propaganda had led its people to believe.

For most of these men, this was a fleeting visit. They would be briefly interrogated and then sent to a secure site somewhere in Britain. They were likely to stay in the palatial quarters of the Gardens for barely a day and night before being loaded onto a military lorry and journeying to a camp, where they would be housed in less inspiring ranks of Nissen huts. Those prisoners would never know the lucky escape they had had. Deemed of little importance to the British intelligence officers, either because they were of too low a rank or just didn't have sufficient, pertinent knowledge to interest the interrogators, they were sent away. Driven in lorries from a building where the grand doors and elegant windows held men subject to torture, threats of death, druggings, beatings and mental humiliation.

The civilians on Kensington High Street knew little of this darker aspect of the Palace Gardens and, even if they had, many would not have cared. If the screams and cries of the men did escape the confines of numbers 6, 7 and 8, it would only be to bounce off the uncaring edifices of other grand buildings and the wavering trees of the avenue.

This was the London Cage. This was Hell in Britain.

An Interview with the Mighty Schottland

If you happened to walk into the London Cage at any time during the war, then it is likely you would have found yourself speaking with a little Scottish man wearing round glasses and smiling genially. Behind polite greetings and good manners he would be assessing your every word. This was Lieutenant Colonel Alexander Scotland, head of the London Cage and an experienced spy and interrogator.

Scotland was a humble-looking man, slightly out of place in the grandiose glamour of his Kensington office. His desk was covered in papers, mostly memos or transcripts of interviews with prisoners; the important details and information about a case were stored carefully in Scotland's own head. He had never had faith in confining all he knew to paper. His knack for gathering intelligence and remembering minor details often proved key in an interrogation; impressing his superiors who had promoted the former working-class grocer to those luxury apartments.

Scotland wasn't there by chance. He had a clear and fundamental understanding of the German war machine, not least because for a short time he had been an honorary supplies officer for the German army. He came to know their methods, their protocols; he understood the German military mind (something that often baffled his colleagues) and he was sharp-witted and a risk taker.

To his German comrades he became Schottland, and he would wander freely among them gathering information. Prior to the First World War, he was already eager to become a British agent and dabbled in espionage. He had a schoolboy spirit about the whole endeavour; even his autobiography reads like a 1930s adventure novel. This was mildly dampened when his German comrades saw through his charade and realised he was a British spy, even if only a minor one. The Germans wanted the British out of South Africa as they ramped up for the First World War and Schottland found himself rotting in a backwater prison.

None of this dampened Scotland's desire to serve his country and his lust for adventure. He served as an intelligence officer during the First World War and then returned to civilian life and travelled extensively between Africa and South America. He quickly realised during his visits that the world was disintegrating into the Second World War. He recognised the rise of Nazism and the threat it posed. Yet despite petitioning the War Office and offering to lecture on the German army, he was politely ignored.

Scotland gives the impression in his writing that he was the only person to realise the approaching danger; of course, he was not, but that attitude sums up his tendency to self-aggrandisement. His most dramatic moment was when he was lured into a trap so that Hitler might interview him. Referred to as Schottland during the chat, which happened in a friend's house, the former spy felt himself in peril of slipping into Nazi clutches and perhaps disappearing forever. When he was finally able to make his exit he was keen to escape; only with hindsight did he see the full extent of the danger he had been in.

Hearing his story tended to leave a chill in the room as listeners realised how easy it was to fall into Nazi snares; to one day be chatting with an old friend and the next vanish in a black car at the hands of the Gestapo. The sinister aspect of the regime was so real and penetrating in Scotland's words that it inspired his underlings. It also might explian why Scotland went on to lose all sympathy for the war criminals in his charge, and why he turned his clever, forward-thinking mind to the practical problem of breaking men and gaining information.

Scotland spoke of the thugs of the SS and the gangsters of the Gestapo, but did not compare them to his own thugs who served as guards and gaolers at the Cage. He denied using torture, while at the same time tacitly suggesting that it happened under his command.

'Once an intelligence man,' he wrote wistfully, 'always an intelligence man.'[1]

Humiliation and Information

Lieutenant Colonel Scotland's Cage was a division of the Combined Services Detailed Interrogation Centre (CSDIC), operating under the auspices of MI-I9 and just under 4 miles up the road from where the War Cabinet met. Opened in the summer of 1940, it ran until 1948, shifting its remit to include German civilians and war criminals.

The staff there were secretive and vague about their work. They quietly followed Churchill's prerogative to do anything to end the war quickly and while other camps stuck in line with the Geneva Convention and operated almost gentlemanly, the Cage interrogators effectively removed themselves from any moral obligation towards humane treatment. They had a goal and nothing would stop them reaching it; they kept just one step ahead of causing their prisoners' deaths, but toyed with all manner of mental and physical abuses. Some would later argue that they were worse than the Gestapo.

Men were broken at the Cage and the staff had developed this into a highly efficient art form. When young aircraftsman Tony Whitehead was sent to the Cage to deliver a particularly unco-operative SS sergeant, he was expecting to find nothing more than a standard military headquarters. Entering the grand entrance hall of the building he was shocked to see a German naval officer scrubbing the floor. The man was wearing full dress uniform and was working on his hands and knees; a burly guardsman casually rested one foot on the prisoner's back while he smoked a cigarette. Whitehead was stunned by the sight, but orders are orders and he left his belligerent captive in the hands of the Cage.

Three days later he returned for his prisoner and discovered a subdued, cowering man. The once arrogant SS sergeant wouldl now not meet his eye and addressed the young aircraftsman as 'sir'. This was almost as stunning as the vision of a naval officer scrubbing the floor. Whatever else may be said for the Cage staff, they were clearly skilled in destroying a man's resolve.

Whitehead might have thought the scene disturbing but he did not voice his doubts until years later. Even if he had felt the urge to say something, what purpose would accosting the guardsman have served? These were hard, tough men, selected from the Guards regiment where they were favoured 'for their height rather than their brains'. Giving orders were ten officers and a dozen NCOs who have been chosen by Scotland.

The Cage had room for sixty prisoners at a time and five interrogation rooms ready for use. Over the eight years the Cage operated, 3,573 men were systematically interviewed and more than 1,000 were persuaded, under psychological pressure, to sign statements on war crimes. The centre got results, which perhaps explains why no one interfered. There were mutterings of concern at the headquarters of the British army in 1946, but only one anonymous Cage officer stepped forward to deal with the issues.

Early in 1946 that officer claimed to have accidentally put the name and location of the Cage on a list of POW camps sent to the Red Cross. The Red Cross was responsible for inspecting any prisoner of war camp and ensuring the requirements of the Geneva Convention were being upheld. They were (and still are) a neutral body that inspected camps in both Britain and Germany, reporting on any breaches. When in 1946 they gained the name of a significant interrogation camp that had been kept secret from them, the Red Cross were, unsurprisingly, keen to make an inspection.

Scotland was furious when a Red Cross inspector called twice at the Cage in March 1946, asking to be let in. On both occasions he was turned away, but a sense of panic began to prevail at the Cage. If the Red Cross entered they were liable to produce a damning report on what they found, and any tacit approval the government had given Scotland would hastily be revoked and denied. Scotland couldn't risk discovery, so he closed ranks and found the officer who had given the game away. The officer promised he would never repeat such a blunder, but Scotland couldn't help wondering if his slip was as accidental as he claimed. One minor addition to a list would ensure that a neutral body could inspect the prisoners and put an end to any harsh practices. Did Scotland think one of his officers had weakened? Did he think, with the war over, the justification of the methods he used on his subjects was being questioned? He never openly discussed the matter, but the close-knit ranks of the Cage had been breached and it was to be the death-knell for the interrogation centre.

Scotland explained his position hotly to the War Office:

The Red Cross has no business coming here, our prisoners are civilians or criminals within the armed forces and they are given no provision under the Geneva Convention. If the Red Cross are allowed to inspect the centre I shall instruct the RAF to no longer send us any man suspected of being involved in Stalag Luft III murders (see below), as the interrogation of these criminals must proceed in Germany under conditions more closely related to police methods than to Geneva Convention principles.

Also, the secret gear which we use to check the reliability of information obtained must be removed from the Cage before permission is given to inspect the building. This work will take a month to complete.[2]

Rattled but defiant, Scotland kept up his obstinate refusal to allow any inspection for a further eighteen months, but even he had to finally concede and a Red Cross inspector was allowed entry. The official found little evidence of abuse but was suspicious that ten prisoners, who were supposedly in an appalling condition, had been moved the night before to other camps. He was also aware that prisoners were afraid to voice complaints in his presence as they had been threatened with reprisals. Angry and feeling deceived, he left the Cage to write the damning report Scotland so feared.

Despite concerns and continuing complaints, the Red Cross chose to do nothing officially as they had been assured the Cage was being closed. They also had valid fears that causing a commotion could be damaging to the interests of the current prisoners. The Cage was in the process of being wound up. Prisoner interrogation was being switched to German internment camps, where, if anything, the treatment was worse.

In 1948 the Cage returned to being three respectable, luxury dwellings for the elite of London. Scotland cleared his desk and left the grand Palace Gardens for the last time, with a view to his retirement. He was contemplating writing a book on his command of the Cage; a justification of its existence and a rebuttal to some of the claims surfacing about brutality at the site. Within two years he was creating his own panic at the War Office when his manuscript appeared for censorship in June 1950. You can almost picture the smile on Scotland's face as he walked down that tree-lined avenue for the final time, plotting a story that would have his superiors running for cover.

Schottland's Case Files

Fascinating as Scotland was, more interesting by far were the people who came through his hands and the methods he used to extract information. Secretive as ever, Scotland was vague about his involvement in significant cases, but the fact remains that the London Cage and similar sites across Britain played host to a number of important war criminals, as well as large numbers of more minor characters.

There was, for instance, The Boy Who Wouldn't Stop Laughing. Captured in 1941, the schoolboy-ish young man was one of a handful of German survivors from the sinking of the *Bismarck* warship. Brought to the London Cage for interrogation, he confounded his questioners by breaking into a fit of uncontrolled giggling every time he was asked a question. No matter how trivial the topic, how simple the query, he would just laugh. Finally, growing frustrated by this strange way of avoiding talking, the interrogation officers handed him over to Scotland. They were still convinced the boy held some vital information, but could not fathom how to extract it.

Scotland approached the interview with his usual lateral thinking and began by questioning the boy on details about his home life, his hobbies, his family, what books he read, what games he played, all in an effort to wrong-foot him. The boy was surprised and somewhat puzzled, yet talked freely enough without resorting to his usual jovial hysterics.

'Then I put to him some point concerning his duties on the *Bismarck*,' wrote Scotland. 'Straightaway the laughter began again. It was as if, for all his childishness, he possessed some intuitive spark, some reflex action, prompting this queer method of avoiding a subject which he had been taught to guard with secrecy.'[3]

Unfazed, as soon as the boy began laughing Scotland joined in. Every time he asked a question he chuckled with the boy, turning the whole episode into 'some rollicking antic between boys, not to be taken seriously'.

Like a catalyst, the jolliness of the conversation suddenly penetrated the boy and abruptly he stopped laughing. The next moment he was discussing in detail his training at a Danzig school for mine specialists. He was one of several young men who had been travelling on the *Bismarck* for sea experience, so many of whom were now drowned at the bottom of the ocean. He was a very lucky survivor and invaluable for his up-to-date information on German mines, which he eventually shared with a British expert on the subject.

A similar instance where Scotland tentatively and persistently drew information from a subject was the *Graf Spee* spy. The case revolved around a Nazi spy ring operating in South America, which regularly sent messages to Germany about the movements of British warships and civilian vessels, enabling U-boats to strike with alarming efficiency at the British shipping supply train.

The *Graf Spee*, a German battleship, served also as a transport vessel for German spies, dropping them in South American ports before carrying on with its other duties. One particular Nazi agent landed at Montevideo. A dark, thickest merchant seaman, he portrayed himself as a civilian passing through and conducted a tour of all the principal ports, speaking with fellow German agents to collect invaluable information for Hitler on Britain's movements. If he had managed to return to Germany there is no knowing what devastation the information he carried could have wrought on the war effort. Fortunately, he was picked up on a Spanish ship during his homeward journey and within a short time he was a guest of the London Cage.

Yet this was no ordinary soldier who could be outmanoeuvred and manipulated into revealing information. He was a well-trained, experienced operative, quite capable of sidestepping questioning and maintaining a façade of ignorance about any useful information.

Once more he fell into Scotland's hands and the unimposing Scotsman, with his soft smile and round spectacles, began his lengthy interrogation. It took fifteen interviews, all patiently and slowly conducted. Scotland knew that if he allowed it to slip how out-dated his own information was then his subject would instantly stop talking. Instead, he maintained his own pretence that he was an expert on the German spy rings in South America. One asset was his better knowledge of the geography of the continent than his prisoner. Before long he had the man resigned to the fact that Scotland was already well informed on all the agents he had visited in South America. Convinced his own information was minor in comparison, he started to talk.

For these cases and many others, Scotland used the basic principles of interrogation: patience and tenacity – techniques that would epitomise British intelligence throughout the war. But there would be other cases where it was rumoured that Scotland lost his patience and resorted to physical and mental torment to succeed. Scotland would always deny this, but the evidence against him and his officers is alarming and compelling.

The Complaint of the Paradis Murderer

The darkest incident involving the London Cage and Lieutenant Colonel Scotland was the holding and interrogation of Fritz Knöchlein, the man who would be later found guilty of the murder of nearly 100 members of the Royal Norfolk Regiment.

The horror of his crimes – considered so despicable, even for the Germans, that two British survivors were not believed when they told their story – was set against a background of torture and brutality that he claimed to have endured at the London Cage. The trial at Hamburg threw Scotland and his team into disrepute; Knöchlein even wrote a lengthy letter on his ill-treatment. Even now, the truth of the matter has to remain a mix of controversy and conjecture.

It all began in 1940. Imagine the pretty meadows of a French peasant farm set in a small, quiet village. It is late May and crops in the fields are growing under a warm, sunny sky. But the red-brick farm buildings are silent and in the distance gunshot is more common than birdsong. The little hamlet of Paradis is just one of many settings for war and, with the German advance looking unstoppable, many have fled or live reclusively in their homes.

The British army is in severe trouble and retreating from the beaches of Dunkirk. Troops are making their slow progress to the coast, fighting all the time, but only doing so to delay the Germans. The war is at its darkest point. A dramatic battle is happening on the La Bassee Canal. The Royal Norfolk Regiment and the Royal Scots have moved into position at Bethune, while on the south side of the canal amass is an SS Totenkopf (Death's Head) Division, one of the most fearsome and evil segments of the army.

As the troops clash in a ferocious and scrappy battle involving hand-to-hand and house-to-house fighting, elderly Madam Romanie Castel and seventeen others flee from the scene and take refuge in a barn at Paradis. Hoping to have escaped the carnage, the eighteen women huddle in the building, little knowing that in a short time they would be witnesses to one of the worst German military massacres of the war.

Thirty-six hours of bitter and piecemeal combat saw the British inflict heavy damage on the Totenkopf, but the SS troops kept returning and they desperately outnumbered the British forces. Their numbers weakened and communications cut off, the Royal Norfolks were pushed back to sleepy Paradis and found themselves confined. On 27 May, as the mass evacuation of Dunkirk took place, the 'A' company of the 2nd Battalion of the Royal Norfolk Regiment prepared for a last stand under the command of Major Ryder.

It was an act of desperate courage. Around a hundred men were gathered in a cowshed on Duries farm, while all around the Germans had set other buildings ablaze. They tried to keep back the advance, but it was soon clear their position was completely lost. The men were ordered to burn documents, destroy equipment, disable any signalling gear and prepare for surrender.

Major Ryder told a sergeant major to tie a white towel to his rifle and to declare their willingness to lay down their arms to the Germans. The sergeant major, with several others, left the cowshed by the rear. Waving the soiled towel, he walked a short way into the meadow. Firing ceased. Germans peered from ditches. There was a moment when it all seemed to be over and the tired and wounded troops felt relief that the ordeal was at an end.

Suddenly, a machine gun opened fire. The sergeant major and some of the men fell and the rest ran for the cowshed. Even now, it seemed, they would not be allowed to give in.

The men waited in silence. There was no further gunfire and, after a while, Major Ryder conceded that perhaps his first intentions were misunderstood. He arranged for another white towel to be attached to a rifle and this time all the men left the cowshed, arms above their heads, except for those supporting wounded comrades.

This time there was no gunfire and the men started to feel relief again. The Germans surrounded them and ordered them down on their knees, with hands on their heads. They were searched for personal belongings and useful documents over the course of the next hour. Some of the men were subject to abusive treatment; rifle butts smashed into faces, men kicked where they knelt. When finally it ended, the men were organised into rows of three and marched further into Paradis.

In her hiding place, Madame Castel heard the sound of a column of men approaching. The women were frightened, some convinced they were about to die, but none dared to look outside. If they did, they would have seen the Totenkopf marching their British captives into another meadow.

In front of a barn they were halted, their backs to the German officers who stood at the gates of the field. The prisoners didn't know what was happening, perhaps some expected another search, or thought they were to be held there for the night. None would have foreseen what was about to occur. Standing at the gate, a German officer shouted, 'Fire!'

Machine-gun bullets laced into the men. Some died instantly, others screamed as they were cut down, bleeding and writhing in the soil. Nearly 100 unarmed men were massacred in a matter of minutes. When the last man fell, some of the Totenkopf were sent over to deal with any survivors. With vicious thrusts of bayonets, anyone who showed a sign of life was slain. Remarkably, despite this, two men escaped the carnage; as the Germans packed up to leave they remained hidden and in agony beneath their fallen comrades.

Madame Castel and the other refugees had heard the sound of the massacre; the screams, the cries and the fall of bodies. Terrified out of their minds, when Germans burst into their hiding place they were now certain death would follow.

One SS officer strode in. He was solidly built, tough, but young for his rank, not yet into his 30s, despite being hardened through his service in concentration camps. His long face was hard, showing not a trace of emotion. Lips tight, he stared at Madame Castel with dark, blank eyes. In the gaze, she felt no hope of being spared.

'Get to your knees!' He screamed at the women, they obeyed. 'What are you doing here?'

'Hiding,' replied Madame Castel.

'Where are you going?'

'I don't know, somewhere away from the fighting.'

'Have you seen any British?'

'Non.'

'Have you been sheltering them?'

'Non.'

'You are a spy! I should kill you!' The officer seemed half-crazed, waving his pistol at Madame Castel, but some essence of common sense came over him, and after a few more minutes of screaming he left the women alone. Later, Madame Castel would stand in a Hamburg court and point out Fritz Knöchlein as this insane SS man, but she was not the only witness against him.

In the bloody meadow Albert Pooley and William O'Callaghan managed to painfully crawl from the pile of bodies. They struggled to a nearby farm and hid in a pigsty. There they were discovered by Madame Duquesne-Creton, who fed and sheltered them. Later, they travelled to Bethune Hospital and became German POWs. Pooley, who has severe leg wounds and was in desperate need of hospital treatment, was quickly repatriated home. O'Callaghan had an arm wound and remained a German captive until the end of the war. Neither man's story arose properly until 1945; they had tried to draw attention to the massacre in 1943, but had been told they had imagined it and were urged to forget it. When Scotland got hold of the story he was stunned and furious that the allegations had not been taken seriously and that there was a real risk the culprits would escape justice.

By 1945, Scotland's team had been renamed as the War Crimes Investigation Unit, swiftly moving from interrogating men on war information to information on war crimes. Scotland began a massive search for men involved in the Royal Norfolk Regiment's massacre. Again and again his officers visited POW camps and looked for SS men who had served with the Totenkopf.

After months of questioning they narrowed down their search to a particular division and to a particular commander – Captain Fritz Knöchlein.

Several Germans came forward, prepared to testify against their former captain. This was highly significant. Those men had declared an oath giving their lives and service to Hitler. The SS oath was unbreakable; men gave up their personal lives and family in favour of the Führer when they joined the division. What happened after that became a secret, only to be known by SS men; to break that sacred pact was an instant death sentence with the SS running their own illegal courts for oath-breakers. No surprise then that Scotland encountered many men too afraid, even with the war at an end, to speak.

Fortunately some did talk, though it took weeks of interrogation to gain the information and to convince them to speak in court. One was Theodore Emke, former member of the Totenkopf machine-gun unit ordered to fire that day. He insisted he was not operating the gun, but saw Knöchlein give the order. Another important witness was Emil Stuerzbecher, an SS lieutenant who could testify about Knöchlein's crazed nature and his determination to shoot any British solider who came into his charge.

With all this against him, Knöchlein finally found himself at the London Cage in October 1946. Stood before the desk of Lieutenant Colonel Scotland, his expression, as always, was stiff and blank, his bearing staunch and upright. Scotland described him as 'full of inhumanity', but it would be Knöchlein who caused the first true outcry against the Cage and questioned Scotland's own humanity.

Scotland always stated that he had no need to interrogate this prisoner; he already had everything he needed, so he made the decision not to even ask for a written statement.

'I wanted no confusing documents with Knöchlein's "version" of events which he could use to try and wriggle out of our net.'

Scotland also made it clear to his guards that he wanted Knöchlein treated especially well: 'This man is extremely precious to us. Everyone here must treat him accordingly. He is to appear in court on a major charge, and I will have nothing said about his treatment in the London Cage which will give him the slightest chance to make a complaint.'

At least that is what Scotland said he told an officer when he was questioned many years later, after Knöchlein's complaint had become well known in official circles. Outside observers might be forgiven for thinking it sounds rather contrived.

Then there is Knöchlein's version of events. In a lengthy letter of complaint he described various tortures he endured:

On the 10th of October 1948, I was brought into the London District Cage … the commandant, Lt. Col. Scotland prescribed the following regulations;

Rations, Breakfast, a half plate of gruel. Noon meal, nothing. Afternoon, one cup of tea. Evening meal, water.

Sleep, one or more guards were continually in my room, or else I had to pass the night in the lavatory while the guards played and sang. Although I was permitted to lie down, there was no question of sleep. This continued for four days and nights.

All my clothing, coat, trousers, shoes, handkerchief, and so forth were taken from me, and a very thin pair of athletic trousers were given me like a sort of pyjamas to wear day and night.

The interrogator was Warrant Officer Ullman who said, and I quote exactly: 'The Alexanderplatz in Berlin is not the only place where Gestapo methods existed. Here we can apply them much better. Here we can smash you up much better. We'll smash you up miserably here. I hate you, I hate you, I have never hated anyone as much as I hate you.'

The guards … had been advised to give me 'adequate' treatment and so … one guard forced me to do 100 trunk-bends, one after the other, without pause, and then other physical exercise to the point where I was staggering. A sergeant who came in interfered in no way. When I tried to stop I was told that it was insubordination and would be punished accordingly. Their remarks were accompanied by continual threats with wooden truncheons.

Then I had to walk around in a circle of the smallest dimensions for four hours continually in the same direction, even though I said I was becoming dizzy and asked at least if the direction could be changed. For this, I received, each time I walked past the guard, a hard kick of his boots in the seat of my pants. Finally I had to turn for so long on my own axis that I could no longer hold myself erect and fell to the floor.

I was put to work with hard labour, mostly of a wholly senseless kind. For example, to scour a staircase, and when I had finished at the bottom to begin again. Senseless scrubbing of the stone floor with a brush (not to clean it); wiping up a large room with a tiny cloth, such as half of a sock; cleaning toilets; hauling coal, despite my pointing out my broken hand joint.

One day I asked continually to be taken to the toilet from 9am to 4pm. Although during this time the guards came into my cell five or six times, they merely laughed, jeering at my request. On another occasion when three of us were squeezed into a narrow little room, so that no one could even move, the guard, in answer to repeated requests to be taken to the toilet, shoved an open pail into the room, inviting us to evacuate into it.

On the 9th November, I was placed in the kitchen beside a multi-flamed gas-range in a corner. The gas flames on which no cooking vessels were standing were turned up very high, so that they gave out a tremendous heat. Then I was forced to scour for one and a half hours a very small piece of wood, without water, without rest, until I was entirely senseless![4]

There is more to the statement than reproduced here, but the examples above are damning in themselves.

Knöchlein wrote his letter with a death sentence looming over him. He was found guilty in Hamburg and Scotland considered the allegations an attempt to escape his execution. Even if Knöchlein could have proved he was forced to confess to the crime, there was no written statement from him and the other evidence against him was too comprehensive to be ignored.

The War Office considered launching an inquiry, but as this would delay the execution and produce no particular result (in their opinion) they decided against it. Knöchlein went to the gallows in early 1948, but he would not be the last to state he had been tortured at the Cage.

The Stalag Luft III Murderers

The most significant role the London Cage had was in the interrogation of several key men involved in the murder of RAF officers who had attempted escape from Stalag Luft III.

One of the accused was Erich Zacharias, a clean-shaven young man with slicked-back blonde hair and hard features. Scotland disliked him intensely, remarking he was 'without doubt the most uncivilised, brutal and morally indecent character in the entire story'.

Zacharias was held responsible for the murders of Royal Canadian Air Force Flying Officer G.A. Kidder and RAF Squadron Leader T.A. Kirby-Green, who had been part of the escape from Stalag Luft III.

Zacharias was bitter about his capture and deliverance at the London Cage, having been betrayed by the wife he had deserted and being further recognised by his portrait painted as part of a mural in a seedy Gestapo night club. It must have seemed an unlikely series of events to lead him to a stately house in Kensington to face murder charges. He was aware his life hung in the balance as he sat before interrogators determined to wrestle the truth from him no matter what.

The Cage staff began their systematic approach on Zacharias. At first refusing to discuss the matter, Zacharias endured beatings and psychological torments to entice him to confess. All the Stalag Luft III culprits suffered starvation, extreme cold showers and the threat of unspecified electrical devices being used upon them. As efficient as ever, the Cage interrogators soon had the men breaking down and signing confessions.

Zacharias was aware of the dangerous position he was in. It was 1947 and Hamburg was organising war trials; whatever promises Hitler had made were long lost as the Führer had taken the easy route out and left his subordinates to suffer the consequences. Zacharias had been a sergeant in the Gestapo Frontier Police, a division that had earned the contempt and hatred of the Allied nations. He had taken part in the shooting of RAF officers, now viewed as national heroes and martyrs, and he was alone. There was no mighty army or powerful dictator to save him. There was not even a true Germany any-more. In that moment, Zacharias' future looked short and depressing.

The guards about him regarded him with unconcealed disgust. They became adept at delivering a sly kick or shove to him as he went past. The cool, calm interrogators were little better. Taking notes and asking question after question, they held little sympathy for the evil young man before them. Scotland had made his feelings clear and they filtered through the ranks.

Zacharias' endurance could only take so much. Beaten and threatened, at some point he had to wonder why he was still holding back. Did he think silence would save him? The British would have their confession one way or another, and refusing to speak only prolonged his ordeal. At least if he confessed he might be free of the Cage. Sitting in one of the stark inter-rogation rooms, he told his story:

It was March of 1944, around four days after the escape. Rumours had it that Hitler was furious about the British prisoners' triumph and had ordered all escapees found and executed. He had eventually been persuaded to retract this and made a marginally more lenient order that only over half the escapees should be shot.

For Zacharias this was a minor change. His orders were simple; to take charge of recaptured escapees and shoot them. The Kripo (criminal police) dealt with finding the men and making the selection of those who would be handed over to the Gestapo for 'interrogation'.

On 29 March 1944 Zacharias travelled with Adolf Knippelberg in a staff car, with drivers Kiowsky and Schwartzer, to collect two men. It was night and Zacharias had sworn his fellows to secrecy with handshakes and oaths to the Führer. This matter was never to be spoken of.

They drove to the local gaol and collected Kidder and Kirby-Green. As the men climbed into the car they had no idea they were about to die. Zacharias took note of his two charges: Kirby-Green was 26 and typi-cally British, with a neat moustache and thick dark hair. He spoke well and Zacharias supposed he was an aristocrat from his suave bearing and stature. Kidder was Canadian and nearly 30, though he gave the appearance of being older. Compared to the tall and slender Kirby-Green he looked stocky with a round, friendly face, high forehead and thicker moustache. Both men were still buoyed by their escape and defiant in front of their cap-tors; Zacharias knew this would all soon change.

They drove to Moravska-Ostrava, part of occupied Czechoslovakia and handily near a crematorium. Zacharias was following his instructions to the letter as he told the driver to pull the car over by the roadside and ordered the two POWs out. Both men were surprised by the turn of events. Pangs of fear began to take hold. Zacharias and Knippelberg, however, had guns and there was no option but to step outside.

It was cold on the roadside and Zacharias only moved the captives a short span away from the road to prevent anything being seen. The drivers stayed by the car to ensure no passers-by stopped and witnessed something they shouldn't. It was now obvious to Kidder and Kirby-Green what was about to happen. They were stopped with their backs to the road, Zacharias close behind. They had mere moments to comprehend the situation, before the young German took aim and shot them both in the back.

'They asked to relieve themselves and then tried to run,' Zacharias nodded to Knippelberg. 'Isn't that right?'

'Yes, they made an escape and we had no choice,' Knippelberg agreed.

Fifty Stalag Luft III escapees would have the same story told about them and used to justify their deaths. Later, the German authorities would become worried that all the Gestapo reports on the shootings were identical and asked the men in charge to vary them.

With the captives dead, Zacharias still had work to do. He sent for a local doctor, who signed their death certificates while nervously watching the two Gestapo officers standing over him with their loaded guns. Then the bodies were rushed to the nearby crematorium and disposed of, before the urns were returned to the Kripo.

Three years later Zacharias found himself explaining this all to a Cage interrogator and writing it out as a confession. He was sent to Hamburg, where all the men on trial complained of torture at the Cage, and Zacharias insisted that he had been beaten and his confession made under psychological coercion.

It would make little difference to the outcome and Scotland viewed it as another Nazi trying to wriggle his way out of the noose. Zacharias was hung on 27 February 1948.

But what was the truth of the Cage? Evidence suggests that at least the threat of torture was present in the gentile Palace Gardens. Yet viewing this with a twenty-first-century mindset and ignoring the context that Scotland worked in risks making history too black and white.

The Cage dealt with the worst of the worst. Men who routinely brutalised and tortured people in their own right, who saw nothing wrong with massacring civilians and unarmed prisoners. Knöchlein had worked in the merciless Dachau concentration camp, where he was a company commandant and regularly killed and beat prisoners. Zacharias was an established Gestapo man with little conscience and no qualms about executing camp escapees. What other crimes he committed in his time in that infamous division we will never know.

While the Geneva Convention and morality stated that these men were no different from other prisoners and should be treated accordingly, can it not be understood that Scotland and his team, angry and frustrated, might resort to physical methods to gain information?

Many in Britain at the time would have felt them justified, many in Germany and France, too. Hatred tends to bury conscience and Knöchlein and Zacharias were two of the most hated men.

We cannot justify the torture. We also cannot state outright that everything Knöchlein or Zacharias said, happened (though it seems likely much of it did). We have to ask ourselves, if we were Scotland, faced with mass murderers who had slaughtered hundreds of innocents without flinching and needed information, would we lose our patience? Would we lose our sympathy? Perhaps even, at our darkest point, our humanity?

Notes
 1 Lieutenant Colonel A.P. Scotland OBE, *The London Cage.*
 2 Ibid.
 3 Ibid.
 4 Fritz Knöchlein, *The London Cage.*

8

POST-WAR INTERROGATION:

BAD NENNDORF

Bad Nenndorf is a small town situated in Lower Saxony, Germany. Founded around the ninth century it has never been a large centre of habitation, and even today its population hovers just over 10,000. At the end of the Second World War, the numbers were considerably less, though bolstered by accommodating the US 84th Infantry Division in its precincts. The town was famous in the eighteenth and nineteenth centuries for its spring water (prior to 1929 it was actually three separate districts, Gross Nenndorf, Klein Nenndorf and the Estate District) and a spa park that was established in 1797. The sulphurous water, which had one time been thought to be the excrement of the Devil, now attracted crowds eager to sample the spring's supposed healing properties. It wasn't long before Bad Nenndorf was one of the most popular German spas and in 1866 it was pronounced the Royal Prussian State Spa and enjoyed the financial support of Berlin.

All that changed with the announcement of war. The spa town was to suffer the usual depredations that hit all of Germany as Hitler dug in his heels and Churchill doggedly defied him. Eventually Bad Nenndorf was occupied by the Americans, but when the war ended the town fell into the British-occupied zone and the darkest patch of the spa's history began.

Mopping-up Duties

Towards the end of the war, as the Allies rapidly encroached on German occupied territory, the various spy agencies veered away from the previous practice of getting agents into Britain and started to concentrate on placing stay-behind agents and line-crossers. By this point, the German secret service was feeling the pinch of defeat and their recruits for espionage now turned into a shabby bunch (with a few exceptions), with poor cover stories and limited skills. Catching them was appallingly easy and they began to create a logistical nightmare.

Stay-behind agents and line-crossers symbolise defensive espionage rather than aggressive. The line-crosser would flit back and forth over the enemy line and report on tactical movements (Lieutenant Colonel Scotland had performed a similar operation in the First World War). The stay-behind agent remained in place while other troops retreated and reported via W/T on the advance of the Allies. Inevitably they would be caught and they were virtually sacrificial in Abwehr minds.

Some of these characters were utterly despicable, both to the Allied minds and to our own, none more so than the hulking traitor Christiaan Antonius Lindemans. Lindemans was a hero of the Dutch resistance movement and had been named 'King Kong' while he served the Allied cause. He was an impressive man of courage, who served the Resistance formidably, killing every German that crossed his path and earning him distinction among his fellows.

Then he was captured. Lindemans was threatened and cajoled, but truly caved when the Germans bargained with him – violence was not his breaking point, but bartering was. The Germans offered to him the release of a brother and sister who had been imprisoned if he would just give information on the Resistance movement. Lindemans agreed and sold out large numbers of the men and women who considered him a hero, including a British officer. It is not clear whether the Germans held up their end of the bargain.

Lindemans' treachery continued, even after being shot in the chest by the Gestapo in 1944, when he corresponded while in hospital with Resistance members and asked for their assistance in an escape attempt. The attempt was obviously a trap created on the Germans' orders and more Resistance members were betrayed and sacrificed by their hero.

Lindemans eventually became a stay-behind agent for the Germans, a role he successfully hid when the Allies overran Brussels. He was still a popular figure and gained an appointment on the staff of Prince Berhard of the Netherlands. He used his role to gain access to even greater information and the British later came to believe that he was responsible for the disastrous blowing of the Arnhem Airborne Operation (1,130 paratroops were killed during the disastrous assault and 6,450 were captured).[1]

Lindemans might have stayed a disguised hero for the Dutch had he not been denounced by a comrade, and in short order he was sent to Ham, England, for the usual interrogations. While there he suffered an epileptic fit and had to be interrogated while under the influence of Luminol, without much gain. In time he broke and the full nature of his treachery was revealed. He could not be executed in England for his treason, but was sent to Belgium for the local authorities to deal with.

It was with a great deal of satisfaction that Lieutenant Colonel Stephens learned, while he was in Bad Nenndorf, that the Dutch hero had taken his own life while residing in an Allied jail.

Traitors like Lindemans made their way to Britain for interrogation via trains and planes, a great effort when fighting a war and, aside from King Kong's tale, not always worth the effort. Feeling like they were drowning in denounced traitors, including supposed communist dissidents who were perceived to be angling for the Third World War, it was decided there was no option but to create interrogation centres on the continent.

CSDIC opened its first European interrogation site at Diest in Belgium. The historic city, with its grandiose architecture and links to the Princes of Orange, seemed an unusual setting: 'The citadel at Diest was on offer and was accepted. It was a mediaeval [sic] sort of place with dungeons and moats and excellently suited for the purpose.'[2] There was some wrangling with the RAF over occupancy of the site and at one point it was even humorously suggested by an officer that the CSDIC would prefer to open their centre in Breendonck, a Belgium fortress with a grisly history of torture. Unfortunately, the officer's words would prove all too prophetic when it came to Bad Nenndorf.

The centre opened in March 1945 (though it had been hoped it would be opened the previous November) and acted as a forward intelligence unit mopping up all those loose ends in Europe. Twelve intelligence officers, four administrative officers and 105 other ranks were gathered from Camp 020, the CSDIC and PWIS (Prisoner of War Interrogation Services). The camp quickly started taking in notables including 'the Beast of Belsen', a man by the name of Kramer wanted by the War Crimes Commission, and Josef Schreieder, a Gestapo official who had worked at the Hague and had intimate knowledge of treachery within the Dutch Resistance (he did not betray Lindemans, however). As the war concluded Diest began to take in men suspected of war crimes and the dimension of the camp changed. Attitudes towards prisoners changed too as a new, grimmer type of man stepped up for interview. Even so, Diest's time at the front line of intelligence would be short-lived and all its 'projects' would be passed on to a newer centre in Bad Nenndorf after September 1945.

Bad Nenndorf

'... is a place of singular charm which has prospered for 150 years on first, second and third class mud. The curative value for the Kraut who suffers from obesity is an admixture of mud and sulphur. The assumption is reasonable that there would be a mountain of residue over the century. Nothing of the kind. They use it over and over again. But the bathrooms lent themselves to prison conversion and that saved many months of basic construction.'[3]

Such was Lieutenant Colonel Stephens' view on the little German spa town where his new centre of operations was set up. When the war ended there was still a tremendous amount of work for the interrogation services to do, from catching, interviewing and trying high-ranking Nazis, to ensuring any plans for rebuilding the Reich or a Third World War were snuffed out as soon as possible. There was also the revival of the threat of communism, which now began to occupy British minds as the government looked warily over their shoulders at their debatable allies in Russia.

Stephens was sent to run the site as he was considered to have the most experience and the most success of breaking suspected spies and terrorists. The site was selected in June 1945, the old baths being requisitioned for the purpose, and on 30 June an advance party of forty-five began the conversion of the leisure spa into a prison, including the usual rings of barbed wire marking the extent of the site. The original accommodation was quite spacious, indicating the large numbers of men the British feared they would have to deal with; however, in practice the buildings were never full and financial restrictions eventually saw the site drastically reduced in size. The place was always in turmoil with reconstruction work and men being demobilised or replaced, making continuity in cases difficult, as well as allowing more naïve treatments to be established when it came to interrogation. Stephens was satisfied, however, that by the time Bad Nenndorf had served its purpose they had developed a 'thoroughly competent organisation'.

In contrast, the Americans had established a similar centre at Oberursel, near Frankfurt, in the old buildings of the German Dulag Luft POW camp, where British and Americans were subjected to heat and suffocation torture to break them. There was no doubt a sense of pleasurable irony at bringing in war criminals to such a place. The British at least had the decency to perceive such reinvention of a Nazi site as crass.

There were four main purposes for Bad Nenndorf: to clear any remaining historical cases, to examine topics of scientific or technical significance, to disrupt any subversive activities within the British zone and to continue counter-intelligence. For the interrogators and the secret service staff who worked there, the war was far from over.

The most important role of these men was to investigate the last days of Hitler in the *Führerbunker*. There was a great deal of confusion about what had exactly happened; the Allies had been preparing for the end of the war and how they would deal with the main Nazi leaders for many months, arguing over the various ways to handle the situation. Churchill would have preferred that certain members of the regime be shot as soon as they were captured and positively identified, but both America and Russia were in agreement that an international trial should be held. Overruled, but reluctant, Britain collaborated to draw up a list of names of the men who would be tried, including Hitler. Churchill still feared that a war trial would give the Führer a chance to spout his Nazi propaganda and, worse, it had the potential for backfiring and enabling him to walk free if the Allies could not prove their case.

That fear was partly relieved when news came out that Hitler had killed himself. The evidence at first was flimsy; it was more rumour than actual fact. Understandably, the Allies were not prepared to stop looking for the worst Nazi of them all until they were absolutely certain he was dead. There was talk that he had escaped to Ireland dressed as a woman, or was hiding out in another of his secret bunkers. Even when the Russians uncovered the bodies of Hitler and Eva Braun they were so badly burned that it took dental records to identify the Führer and the trust Britain placed in its eastern European ally was limited. Eventually, witnesses to the suicide and the later burning of the bodies were discovered, and they convinced the officials that Hitler was indeed dead. But there was now another fear; Hitler had supposedly sent emissaries from his bunker carrying his will and political testament and a message for the resurrection of the Nazi creed. The CSDIC in Bad Nenndorf now put its efforts into tracking down these documents as quickly as it could.

The number of emissaries, the number of copies of the documents and where they could all be found was the first investigative step. The initial breakthrough did not occur at Bad Nenndorf, but at a camp in Fallingbostel, where a German press official, Lorenz, who had been in the bunker, was taken and interviewed. He had escaped from the bunker on 29 April and evaded arrest up until 25 May when he was caught in Hannover going under the pseudonym of George Thiers. He conceded his real identity relatively quickly, but it was many months before it was discovered that he had typed copies of Hitler's and Goering's testaments sewn into his jacket. He would not talk on the subject to the camp staff, so he was duly transferred to the new CSDIC centre at the German baths on 17 November. It took twelve days to break him and the result was gratifying.

Lorenz told that he was one of three emissaries that he knew of; his own documents had been given to him by prominent Nazis Martin Bormann and Goebbels, and his orders were to take them to Admiral Doenitz who had replaced Hitler, or, if that was impossible, to have them published for historical posterity. The other recipients were Standartenführer Zander, who was to take Hitler's political and personal testaments, along with the Führer's marriage certificate, to Doenitz and Major Johannmeyer, who was also given a copy of Hitler's political testament and possibly his personal one too.

This was a big triumph for the British interrogators, not least because they had beaten the Americans to this nugget of information (and there was always a friendly rivalry between the two countries' secret services). After running all their own checks on the documents to determine their authenticity, they were handed to the Americans, who ran their own analysis before agreeing that they could be released to the press.

Another Nazi helped to clarify the story and provide confirmation of Lorenz's evidence; his name was von Below, and he had been a personal adjutant to Hitler since 1937. A fanatical Nazi, he was of significant intelligence value and when he was captured masquerading as a student at the University of Bonn it was with enthusiasm he was sent before a team of non-CSDIC interrogators. They were inexperienced and their zeal detracted from their effectiveness. Von Below remained stubbornly unco-operative and one novice interrogator even came to believe that the man did not hold any useful information because he could not get it out of him. He concluded he was a 'straightforward person' and washed his hands of the case.

By the time von Below reached Bad Nenndorf and the experienced interrogation team under Stephens' watch, he had become stubbornly entrenched in his silence and determined not to talk. This was a typical hazard of failed interrogations; it caused the suspect to shut down further and draw confidence in his silence. The first efforts to break him, despite a strong intelligence section working on the case, failed. It was only after a second effort and considerable difficulty that von Below was broken and he revealed the truth, that he had been given two letters before his exit from the bunker, one from Hitler and the other from General Krebs. Because he had been unable to deliver them and feared them falling into Allied hands, he had burned them, but not before he had read the contents. The Bad Nenndorf interrogators pushed for him to give a summary and extracts from the reconstructed Hitler letter are below:

> The fight for Berlin is drawing to a close. On the other fronts as well the end can be expected within a few days … I am going to commit suicide rather than surrender … two of my oldest supporters, Goering and Himmler, have broken faith with me at the last minute … my trust has been misused by many people … disloyalty and betrayal have undermined resistance throughout the war. It was therefore not granted to me to lead the people to victory … the efforts and sacrifices of the German people in this war have been so great that I cannot believe they have been in vain. The aim must still be to win territory in the East for the German people.[4]

Of course, how much of this was Hitler's words and how much von Below's interpretation of them remains open to debate, but the interrogators were convinced the phrases rang true and sounded genuine. Indeed it sounds the sort of letter a defeated Führer would write, and it is probable the majority is an accurate statement of the original letter.

Von Below was also able to confirm that there had only been three copies of Hitler's will, or at least those were all he had seen in Berlin. He was shown a copy of the one found on Lorenz and agreed that it matched the originals he had witnessed. Yet another triumph and the nail in the Reich coffin was hammered home.

The Allies would receive their last nugget of information from a rather unusual Nazi test pilot, Hanna Reisch. Remarkable for being a successful female test pilot (she survived being encased in a V1 rocket as a human check on the gyroscopic system when all seven of her predecessors had suffered broken spines upon crash-landing); she had also saved Goering's successor Greim's life when he was flying to Berlin. A truly courageous person, she filled in the gaps for the British, but she was held by the Americans and not at Bad Nenndorf, so reference to this extraordinary lady can only be in passing.

Viva Italia

It was not just the German wartime leaders the interrogators were interested in at Bad Nenndorf; the British were tieing up all loose ends and this included some Italian events prior to the country's co-operation with the Allies. In particular, the Bad Nenndorf interrogators were set the challenge of unravelling the story of the liberation of Mussolini in September 1943.

Mussolini had fallen foul of the Italian King Victor Emmanuel III, as well as many of his political colleagues, when Italy's war effort began to look particularly bleak and the country was in crisis. Moves were afoot to return full power to Victor Emmanuel and remove Mussolini. By July 1943 the Grand Council of Fascism had voted with a 19-7 margin that the king should return to his full constitutional power, and within a day of the vote Mussolini (who never truly took the vote seriously) was arrested.

He was removed in secret and put into hiding as it was well known that the Germans would not like the decision and would probably try to rescue him. Mussolini was replaced by Marshal Pietro Badoglio who, while putting up pretence of supporting the Nazi war effort, was in reality negotiating peace with the Allies. The Germans, however, knew that without Mussolini Italy would not remain a supportive war ally for long and plans were afoot to rescue the once great dictator, which they eventually succeeded in.

For the British and the new Italian governors this was a dangerous political event, as Mussolini could stir up future trouble. Throughout the war he remained at large, though his heart was no longer in politics and he was little more than a puppet for Hitler. He was spotted by partisans in April 1945 as he was trying to get to Switzerland with his mistress where a plane would take them to Spain. He was gunned down, yet British interest still remained in his liberation, and as part of Bad Nenndorf's remit was to examine historical cases it was logical that Mussolini's rescue would be on their list of interrogation topics.

It was the interrogation of Otto Sweert, a German lieutenant who had taken part in the rescue of Mussolini, that finally revealed what had happened in September 1943. Sweert worked for Skorzeny, who, in 1943, was the SS obersturmführer, and who has become the name synonymous with Mussolini's liberation. Skorzeny sent his lieutenant to Rome to join a Kommando unit consisting of thirty men recruited from various SS Sonderkommandoen groups.

The operation of rescuing Mussolini had the potential for such severe repercussions that it was kept a closely guarded secret; even Sweert's new unit initially knew nothing of their ultimate goal. With Italy lying about its allegiances and shaking hands with the Allies, while saluting the Nazis on their doorstep, the air of mistrust was immense and Skorzeny chose to keep his troops in the dark. The Kommando unit helped in the disarmament of Italian troops in early September and a few days later learned from Skorzeny of their real mission. Sweert now began to take charge; he had to pick the fittest men in the unit and get a car ready. There were to be eleven gliders towed by planes used in the operation; four planes would be occupied with parachutists, who were to secure the plateau on which the hotel where Mussolini was held prisoner sat. The crews of two more planes, one of which would be piloted by Skorzeny, were to storm the hotel and take Mussolini unharmed. Five remaining units had the task of occupying the railway station and seeing that the former six planes achieved their given tasks.

The general in charge of watching Mussolini was arrested by the SS and interrogated; Skorzeny insisted that he was to be persuaded to help voluntarily to prevent 'unnecessary' bloodshed. But the SS reputation for torture leaves room to wonder if physical devices were not used against the unfortunate general. Whatever the case, the general eventually talked and was even taken in a plane so he could point out the location where Mussolini was being kept. Cryptically, Sweert explained the Italian was persuaded by the commander of the unit giving 'his word of honour that nothing would happen to him'.[5]

At 11.15 p.m. on the night of the liberation the eleven planes, with their attached gliders, each holding nine men, set out. There was no wireless communication between the aircraft and the dark night made it nearly impossible for planes to see each other. The plane carrying the Italian general landed 50yds from the hotel and the men rushed into the dining room of the building. Mussolini was not there, so they carried on to the telephone and telegraph room where the communication cables were cut. Skorzeny now arrived and together they climbed a wall into the yard of the hotel, much to the surprise of a company of Italian soldiers. In the commotion that naturally followed, an upstairs window flew open and the erstwhile Italian leader looked out.

Skorzeny rushed to Mussolini, while Sweert was left in command of the men, organising the disarming of remaining Italian troops and the securing of the hotel. Communication was established with the railway station the other aircraft had been sent to secure. and in a short time an aircraft arrived and escorted Skorzeny and Mussolini (who was rather cool about his German rescue) to Germany.

Mussolini may have escaped falling into Allied hands but it was not a happy liberation. His health had suffered from the strain of captivity and Italy's failing war effort. He had no stomach left for fighting either alongside or against the Germans and would have preferred to retire from the war altogether. Hitler had other plans. He knew Mussolini remaining as the head of Italy was the only way he could keep the country on side, so he set about persuading the aging Fascist leader to set up a new party, which could eventually return him to power. His persuasion involved calm threats involving the wholesale destruction of massive parts of Italy should Mussolini refuse.

For his part, Otto Sweert returned to Germany and was decorated for his success, but his medal could not overshadow the horrors he inflicted on others and he was eventually convicted of war crimes in Denmark and hanged. When he arrived at Bad Nenndorf it was with knowledge of this fate hanging over him, and he made at least half a dozen attempts to escape the old spa. At one point he made a spectacular breakout; cracking the bars on his window and climbing over and through several strings of defences to end up in a nearby village. CSDIC was frantic to find him; the escape of a convicted war criminal would not only make a mockery of the proud British security at the site, but disgrace the intelligence teams. Searches were extensive, but Sweert was not one of the ill-prepared or foolish Abwehr recruits CSDIC had dealt with at Ham. He obtained a full set of new clothes from a villager and almost slipped unnoticed into the community. His disguise, however, was not convincing enough and after twelve hours of freedom he was recaptured, much to the delight of CSDIC.

Science and Subversives

The Allies knew that Germany, despite its unrelenting campaign against Jewish academics and scientists, had spent large portions of its wartime funds on various experiments, both technological and medical. The aim of all this was usually the development of some super-weapon or the improvement of care and safety of the armed forces. Concentration camps provided a ready source of guinea pigs and when they were not studying the effects of a faulty Typhus vaccine at Buchenwald, they were experimenting with the effects of extreme cold and lack of oxygen on the human body (supposedly to help German sailors and pilots survive crashes and accidents).

Rumours (sometimes deliberately spread) filtered into the Allies' ears at regular intervals about the breakthroughs the Germans were making, and at the end of the war the biggest concern was to discover truth from fiction and confiscate any dangerous material before it could reach Russian hands. The shipping to England of scientists involved in the Atomic bomb race has already been mentioned as a way to avoid such significant information being claimed by the Soviets, who were considered to be already making their own war plans.

Initial information on the 'techno-industrial organisers of the Nazi era' came from a civil servant held at Bad Nenndorf, named Landfried. The elderly Landfried initially tried the old ruse of memory loss due to shock when faced with his interrogators, but as it became more apparent that Germany was finished and his survival relied on British clemency, he started to talk; finishing his interrogations with the all too familiar plea that he would now like to be a 'good European' for the sake of Germany's future. Alongside him was Vageler, a specialist in colour photography for aerial photography. He was a genius at geological surveys and a man of high ambition (he had taken a deep interest in the development of the German Colonial Organistion that was designed to govern British, French and Belgian colonies at the end of the war), but unfortunately he was also an ardent Nazi. The information he gave on technical and scientific concerns had both the Americans and the British chomping at the bit to interrogate him, and he was eventually removed from Bad Nenndorf to a place where experts could listen to the information he gave.

A side-note of Bad Nenndorf history was the discovery of a swindle both by and against the Nazis. Phillip Reemtsma was a German tobacco tycoon of flexible ethics who was blacklisted by the Nazi Party because of his illegal remission of tax debts. Unfazed, Reemtsma turned to that other Nazi swindler, Goering, and bought him with a 'donation' of 4 million marks and a promise of an annual contribution of 1 million marks. So successful was this corruption that Reemtsma's personal income rose from 525,455 marks in 1933 to 6,048,137 marks in 1934 and 59,794,912 marks in 1941! Who knows what would have happened had his clever dealings been discovered by less corruptible members of Hitler's regime. As it was, Lieutenant Colonel Stephens wrote with some satisfaction 'that his luxurious home in Hamburg is [now] a British Officers' country club'.

Technology might have proven a fascinating and useful sideline of interrogation, but it did have the ring of fear and potential for disaster about it, as did the investigation of subversives and those angling for the Third World War. Even before the war ended, Britain and America had known there was a danger that elements within Germany would band together to rebuild the Reich and force another war. Generals in captivity were diligently recorded in secret discussing an early end to the war so that forces could be regrouped and prepared for the next attempt. Britain had been sifting its prisoners from fairly early in the conflict, classifying them for their political leanings and assessing those who posed the greatest risk to peace. America had been less stringent and, as the war ended, had found on their hands large hubs of hardcore Nazis itching to get home and talk strategies. America, closely followed by Britain, instigated re-education programmes to reduce radical Nazism. Meanwhile, in occupied Germany the intelligence agencies of the two Western Allies worked together to shut down any potentially dangerous political movements.

We might think today of MI5 routing out revolutionaries such as the IRA and Al Qaeda as part of their daily routine, but that is nothing compared to the terrifying threat felt at the end of hostilities; the fear that ranks of men were massing to lay plans for another war. For Britain, still licking its wounds and wondering about the Soviet Union's future plans, such a thought could dredge up deep-rooted nightmares and memories of the failure to hobble Germany's military might sufficiently after the First World War. With this in mind, Bad Nenndorf became part of a system to monitor and close down any subversive movements.

One organisation, an off-shoot sponsored by former leaders of the Hitler Jugend, came to attention in the last months of 1945 when its threat potential started to dramatically rise. The purpose of the new group was simple – the resurrection of the Nazi creed. Ten million marks had already been sunk into the cause and the members were working to establish cells and infiltrate places such as schools where their views could be permanently embedded in the minds of the young – the Hitler Youth, after all, had proven how successful these tactics could be. A network of document forgers was created and plans were underway to remove the dangerous SS tattoo marks on some of the members.

The British and Americans worked jointly on an operation code-named 'Nursery', with US intelligence infiltrating the organisation, which by December 1945 was considered too dangerous to exist any longer. The two occupied zones pounced around the same time. The Americans made arrests in the same month, while Britain took its first captives in January 1946. Now, two ringleaders, Budaus and Lohel, were sent to Bad Nenndorf.

The two Germans were stubborn with the courage of fanatics as they faced the interrogators, but their initial silence did not last long and when they broke it was with dramatic results. Indeed, combined with the denunciations of eleven more of their colleagues, the Allies found themselves with 600 names of supporters who had intimate and damning ties with the group. Just quantifying the data needed an army of typists; the report was reduced (with difficulty) to a slightly more concise document of 200 pages.

This was far from the only operation the interrogators at Bad Nenndorf were involved in. There were operations 'Lampshade', 'Deadlock', 'Globetrotter' and 'Brandy'; and it wasn't just Germans that were making the British itch with anticipation, the Russian threat that would eventually slip into the Cold War was already being felt and suspected communists were being rounded up and shipped to Bad Nenndorf as rapidly as former Nazis.

This constant attack, threats and dangerous political movements took its toll on Stephens. When it came to Bad Nenndorf he still achieved his breaks, but he fundamentally believed that hope of a peaceful future was lost. In a telling passage, probably written as he sat in the former bath buildings, said everything about his bitter, bleak outlook:

> … only a label distinguishes the German democratic parties from the normal subversive small organisations every Secret Service must watch. Indeed these parties are already corrupt … The Germans are not impressed by the democratic way of life and they will turn to their 'One Party' system just as soon as the occupation ends. Deep down in the German mind it is not the Nazi creed that has failed, but rather the leadership, which did not produce world domination. One day the patient, inarticulate mass will again throw up a demagogue. He will be no leader, just a radical opportunist … then war will come again; only the time factor is an issue, and that is dependent upon the circulation of the atomic bomb.[6]

Stephens' dark views could not have been helped by the growing evidence of Russian espionage in the British zone, which was a far cry from the befuddled scrambling in the dark of the Abwehr. One shrewd informer told that most Russian officers were anticipating war with the Western Allies and that there would be no more polite handshakes between Churchill and Stalin; already spurious rumours were flying that it was only the Russians who had done any serious fighting against the Germans. The way they saw it, the great America and Britain sat back and watched while the Red Army dealt the Nazi death-blow. If that wasn't bad enough, the Western Allies had swooped in and claimed the benefits and territory won by Soviet military. Even darker stories that the Allies were actively supporting fascism and were intent on creating a bloc against the USSR had men tossing in their sleep. The distrustful rot had set in and nothing would stop it now.

The Russians were confounding their betrayal by trying to stir up further German hatred against the West. One spy, on being interrogated, revealed that propaganda meetings were being held in the armaments factories of Depper & Sons in Dresden. Orchestrated by Russian officers, the theme of the meetings was to reinforce the inevitability of a war between Russian and the Western democracies. Spouting how the British would soon be fleeing across the Channel, the speakers made it crystal clear that very soon the Red Army would be dominating the world, and only with their aid could Germany reunite into some semblance of its former self. The Germans would have to look to the Russians for their salvation; a grim prospect and one most Germans would have dreaded more than death.

But the Russian revolutionaries and spies were adamant – their creed would soon wipe out Western capitalism and communism would rule a new world due to their superior military skills and might. There was even an attempt to infiltrate the CSDIC, first with an agent named Albrecht and then, when he failed, with a 17-year-old girl named Sonja Broschinski. The Russians believed her youth would prevent the British holding her, though how they hoped she could achieve success remains mystifying; she failed as well.

Some of the Russian spies were German born, having been recruited by the industrious propaganda agents. They included Gleich and Wilhelm, who had both used W/T in the German armed forces, but when recruited had to serve another seven to eight months with the Russians training on the same technology. They were also exposed to political indoctrination, with the lieutenant colonel of their training centre giving regular talks on politics, consisting of the right amount of scorn for Western democracy and high praise for Bolshevism.

Wilhelm needed little of this propaganda as he had already worked as a Russian agent against the Germans during the war. He was given the mission of setting up a spy network and recruiting a German girl, who would in turn seduce and marry a British soldier so she might continue her espionage work in England. Ambitious indeed! Perhaps Wilhelm considered it too ambitious, because he voluntarily surrendered to the British authorities, and Gleich was not far behind. They were but the tip of the iceberg and the British intelligence knew that many more of their ilk had stayed loyal and were working for the Russians within the British zone.

Polish and Russian authorities were slipping men and women in under the guise of official channels; the British zone was distinctly compromised.

No wonder that Bad Nenndorf examined some 350 cases in its time, compared to 400 in the CSDIC centre at London and 480 at Ham. It was obvious the end of the war had not changed anything for the interrogators. In fact, their work pressure was about to increase.

Double Standards

'They were subjected to mental torture and physical assault during the interrogations ... Guards had been instructed to carry out physical assaults on certain prisoners with the object of reducing them to a state of physical collapse and of making them more amenable to interrogation.'[7] As Mark Thiessen quoted in his recent book entitled *Courting Disaster*, a work that has proved controversial with some of its pro-torture views and suspect history. The quote is supposedly from a briefing to British Foreign Secretary Ernest Bevin in 1946 on Bad Nenndorf and his book, along with other new claims, has cast a shadow on the secret dealings of the British interrogators.

Could it really be that Lieutenant Colonel Stephens, who so vehemently spoke out against torture and even banned fellow interrogators who used rough methods, went against his own ethos? The evidence is not confined to controversial books (Mark Thiessen was soundly criticised by Jane Mayer in *The New Yorker*, but then the full title of his book does call for a degree of backlash), The National Archives also list an array of documents concerned with conditions at Bad Nenndorf. Inquiries were held and several members of staff were court-martialled, including Stephens. What went so horribly wrong?

Torture, as has been mentioned in an earlier chapter, tends to be the tool of the inexperienced. It is not a productive method and it reeks of laziness and desperation; it makes no leeway for the wrong man being accused. Instead, once started upon, it tends to escalate out of an interrogator's own fear of being wrong. Once this has happened there is no going back.

The turnover of staff at Bad Nenndorf was far too high for consistency to be maintained; from an intelligence perspective it worried Lieutenant Colonel Stephens immensely, from a humanitarian perspective it was disastrous. Interrogators needed to work in a close-knit, unified group. They needed to trust one another and their methods and, as mentioned earlier, they tended to become a closed society where new individuals were distrusted. This unity had its good and bad points: at the London Cage it enabled torture to be covered up, at Camp 020 it prevented it. At Bad Nenndorf that close system of trust and comradeship was not possible when men were being demobbed and sent home to be replaced by inexperienced novices.

The best interrogators were leaving, men who had had an entire war to hone their skills, and they were replaced with a mismatch of substitutes from various branches. Stephens had previously run a tight camp at Ham, he had had full control over his men and their methods, but now his team was being systematically dismantled and new men from different divisions were being drafted in. There was no knowing what methods these men had used in their earlier CSDIC camps. If they had any connection to the London Cage then there was reason to be suspicious, but even if they didn't, the pressure being applied both from the higher ranks and the underlying fear circulating post-war Germany to break into the communist spy rings left interrogators resorting to grotesque methods for results.

There is no denying that Gestapo methods were at times meted out within the camp, and it seems Stephens had taken a back seat, shut his eyes even. His control of the camp was nowhere near the level he had once held at Camp 020. Instead, he was busy revising the history of Ham ready for publication and his interrogators were left to their own devices.

News of the harsh treatments broke sooner than the interrogators had presumably expected. They were incredibly foolish (another mark of their ignorance); they dumped half-dead, starving prisoners outside a military hospital as if hoping the ill-treatment would not be traced to the CSDIC centre. A Royal Artillery officer complained about the state of the inmates, some weighing less than 6st and two dying after arrival.

How the Bad Nenndorf staff thought they could get away with such obvious maltreatment beggars belief – this was not Nazi Germany and they were not the actual Gestapo who could rely on officials turning a blind eye. But it could be argued that they had become blinded by the power they held over these men, power held at a safe distance from England in an occupied and defeated Germany. By now turnover at the camp had become so bad that some of the warders were ex-convicts – the only ones left to serve the centre – and standards were falling dangerously.

As early as 1946, others began to raise their voices in protest. Captain Arthur Curtis, a naval officer commanding an internment camp where inmates of Bad Nenndorf were sent after the interrogators had finished with them, was so stunned by the state of men entering his care that he had photographs taken to back up his claim of them being little more than living skeletons. Those photographs, which still exist, show young men starved to the point that nearly every bone is visible. Hip bones stand out starkly and spines are clearly defined down their backs. Some look stunned and shell-shocked by their ordeal, gazing out of the picture with the looks of madmen; others still sit tall and glower at the photographer, determined to weather this storm as well.

They could just have easily been the victims of a concentration camp, except they were not Jews, but suspected communists; their captors not evil SS men, but supposedly decent British officers. By now the camp's remit was shifting from Nazi war criminals to Russian spies; men who were once supposed to be Allies and many of whom were innocent of the charges levelled against them. The feeling of panic in the air started to come through.

Back in Britain the public and the government were outraged. A Scotland Yard detective, Inspector Tom Hayward, was called in by senior army officers to investigate Bad Nenndorf and get to the bottom of these claims. Hayward's report was damning. One of the men he talked to was Gerhard Menzel, a 23-year-old student who had been arrested by British intelligence in June 1946. He fell under the loosest of suspicions due to having travelled from Omsk, Siberia (where he had been a POW) to the British zone. It wasn't a lot to go on, but then Stephens had always talked about intelligence 'hunches' that brought a man into his care. Presumably Menzel had been just such a hunch.

Menzel told Hayward that during his time at Bad Nenndorf he had been treated appallingly. His hands had been restrained behind his back for up to sixteen days at a time, and while unable to protect himself he had been punched in the face repeatedly. He spent long periods in a freezing cold room, sometimes up to two weeks, during which time he was doused in cold water every half an hour from 4.30 a.m. until midnight. Hayward discovered this was a common method used on the men.

When Menzel was sent to an internment camp eight months later, his condition was horrendous, his weight was only 7st 10lbs. He could neither stand nor walk without assistance and spoke with great difficulty as his lips and tongue were swollen and split. It was impossible to take his body temperature as it was under 35°C and the thermometer only started at 35°C. Menzel was confused, anxious and suffering acute memory loss. His blood pressure had sunk so low the doctors deemed it dangerous and his lungs were infected – probably with pneumonia considering the conditions he had been in. After washing him, feeding him and warming him with heat lamps the doctors managed to drag his temperature up to 36.3°C, but things did not look promising for Menzel's survival.

He had arrived with twelve other former Bad Nenndorf inmates, all just skin and bones and dressed in the ragged remains of their clothing. They were not the first batch the internment camp had seen in this state, and aside from being emaciated men had facial scars from beatings and scars on their shins, which rumours held were due to shin screws the British had retrieved from a Gestapo prison in Hamburg.

Another young man, Heinz Biedermann, was a 20-year-old clerk arrested while he was in the British zone because his father lived in the Russian zone and was considered an ardent Nazi. He was detained in October 1946. Four months later, when he was shipped to an internment camp, his original weight of 11st 3lb had dropped to 7st 12lb. He complained of being held in a freezing room barely clothed, facing constant threats of execution and suffering solitary confinement for most of the time. It was like life under the Nazis all over again; say the wrong thing, be related to the wrong person, and you were doomed.

Other inmates of Bad Nenndorf included a helpful young German who had offered to spy for the British in the Russian zone, but had been mistrusted over an error on his medical records (this – though not his treatment – was understandable considering the number of enemy agents who tried to infiltrate the CSDIC in such a way). A tragic case was that of the homosexual ex-soldier who had attempted to enter the British zone with false papers to find his lover. He starved to death at Bad Nenndorf. The list just carries on: some of the victims were innocent, some were indeed spies or war criminals, but within a matter of months Bad Nenndorf was viewed with disgust and scorn. Stephens' former, untarnished record of cordiality to prisoners now hung in the balance. One camp guard told Inspector Hayward he had complained that Stephens and his comrades were behaving as badly as the Germans, which made him extremely unpopular, especially with his sergeant.

However, it would take until 1948 for the authorities to move and four British officers to face courts martial. In April of that year the second of the courts martial began, with the accused being the medical officer at Bad Nenndorf, Captain J.S. Smith. The trials were largely kept behind closed doors, but Smith must have felt relatively confident as in the previous case his colleague had been acquitted; a medical man must surely stand a similar chance, especially as he was concerned with the care of prisoners not the interrogation.

The main witness against him was Count Buttlar-Brandenfels, who had a catalogue of abuses to launch at him, including 'the loss of four toes to his treatment in a freezing punishment cell last winter while he was held for interrogation by the British Intelligence Service'.[8]

As a medical officer, Smith should have ensured the count did not suffer such injuries, but his defence counsel had a few tricks up their sleeves, the main one being to prove Buttlar-Brandenfels was an outright liar.

'Do you know that your intelligence file describes you as a liar of truly gargantuan proportions?'[9] Mr Slade, the defence for Smith, accused the injured German. He went on to argue that he had been visited by Smith nine times while he had been a prisoner at Bad Nenndorf and never once had he specified, *in writing*, that he was having problems with his toes. The defence was almost laughable! That they actually thought that failure to write down the problem could excuse Smith sounds ridiculous, but Slade had another line of defence. He turned on Buttlar-Brandenfels and called him a malingerer of the worst kind. With a spark of wit that cut through Slade's arguments, the count snapped back: 'Would I malinger four of my toes off?'

He also hotly argued against Slade's suggestion that he had malingered his way out of the German army and had at one time been a part of the Gestapo. He had never been in the army at all, he snapped, and he had in fact been arrested by the Gestapo, a far cry from working for them. As for a supposed slip one night when he had told an interrogator he was a Gestapo man, it had merely been the result of a high fever and delirium.

These side-swipes from Slade were not helping his client. When he started to harangue a second witness, Dieter Albrecht, who was describing being left naked in a cold punishment cell, Slade called the evidence irrelevant to the case as there was no proof that the cruelty had been brought to Smith's attention. He was overruled by the deputy judge-advocate-general who considered the report relevant as it showed the conditions within the camp.

Smith was to be unlucky; out of the four court-martialled officers he was the only one to be convicted. He was found guilty of professional neglect (though acquitted of manslaughter) and his sentence was to be dismissed from the army.

So what of Lieutenant Colonel Stephens? He was one of the four charged officers and faced accusations of professional negligence and disgraceful conduct, the latter charge being dropped on the first day of the trial due to insufficient evidence. Most of Stephens' trial was to be conducted behind closed doors as some of the material and several of the witnesses required protection from spying Soviet eyes. A number of high-profile figures came to his defence, including Sir Dick White, who would become a future head of MI5 and MI6.

Stephens pointed out his reputation for standing steadfast against the use of physical violence; he had even petitioned unsuccessfully for an increase in rations at the camp. He had been fighting a difficult battle, he claimed: his staff was cut from 700 to 330, but quick results were still expected. It also had to be kept in mind, he added, that Bad Nenndorf was not designed to be a cosy place, it was a tough prison for tough prisoners, many of whom were being interrogated for war crimes and were the worst kind of Nazis. There were even men there who had implemented the Holocaust. Mental pressure in many forms was used to break the prisoners, though Stephens swore he had prohibited the use of violence. He had even distributed copies of *A Digest of Ham* to the camp interrogators to demonstrate the success of non-violent methods.

Stephens reiterated to the court why, to him, torture was an inadequate and slapdash method. He argued that it produced quick answers to please, not necessarily accurate or honest ones, and it did not induce a prisoner to be conversational. It also had the serious problem of causing a public back-lash (as they were now experiencing), which could only be detrimental to the intelligence services.

Stephens' reputation went a long way to proving his case and ulti-mately he was acquitted, though it is still hard to see how so much misery could have gone on without coming to his attention. We can only assume

Stephens was blind to the problems at his camp for a number of reasons, not least the staffing difficulty, the Nuremburg Trials (which stole away some of his captives) and the ongoing issues with communism. The abuses slipped under his radar, which in itself was a failing of the mighty 'Tin-Eye'.

If anything positive could be seen to come from the Bad Nenndorf case it was the highlighting of the need for stricter controls and practice within interrogation centres. The British government did not want a repeat of the case that brought everyone into disrepute, so protocols and guidelines were set up and are still enforced within MI5 today. Stephens' words about the perils and dangers of torture still resonate today, too; it is saddening that the lessons of the Second World War have failed to be appreciated by some: there are those within supposedly civilised organisations that believe in physical force as a worthwhile tool. Torture did not work for the Germans or the Russians, it certainly didn't work for the Allies, so why is it still used today? That is a subject for another book and as long as there are those that condone it and even endorse it, then even Stephens' decisive words on the subject will not change that. We still have our Bad Nenndorfs, they just don't happen to be in Germany any more.

Notes

1 'Airborne Troops Retreat from Arnhem', *On This Day: 26 September 1944*, BBC News *http://news.bbc.co.uk/onthisday/hi/dates/stories/september/26/newsid_3523000/3523972.stm*.
2 Lieutenant Colonel Stephens (ed.), *A Digest of Ham*.
3 Ibid.
4 Ibid.
5 Ibid.
6 Ibid.
7 Mark A. Thiessen, *Courting Disaster: How the CIA kept America Safe and How Barack Obama is Inviting the Next Attack*, Regnery Publishing Inc., 2010.
8 'Alleged Malingerer at Bad Nenndorf', in *The Times*, Tuesday, 13 April 1948.
9 Ibid.

Chained Lions:

Characters of the Interrogation Files

So many figures of the Second World War passed through interrogation services that the files start to look a bit like a 'who's who' of wartime culture. Nazis, war criminals, double agents, spies and the significant men who interviewed them have all been recorded in ways that are a treasure trove to historians. The interrogation records are not a carefully drafted letter or speech, a cleverly edited biography or a sharply penned memoir; they are straightforward, insightful records of the men and women who played their lives out on the Second World War stage. Nothing can be more candid, nothing more revealing, than the direct conversations of these figures. When all the official trappings are stripped off them, when all there is are questions and answers, then they stand starkly before us; their characters, good or bad, exposed. We would, therefore, be remiss not to pause and look at what the files tell us in broader terms about the personalities of the Second World War.

The Team Leaders – Stephens and Scotland

It would be impossible to miss that the main players throughout these pages on the Allies' side have been Lieutenant Colonel Stephens and Lieutenant Colonel Scotland. Men of very different natures and temperaments who shaped Second World War interrogation; their own lives, however, shaped them and it was through their experiences that they came to develop inter-rogation as we know it today.

Stephens was the smart, upright, proud soldier. Nicknamed 'Tin-Eye' for his fondness of wearing a thick monocle, he was known as something of an odd extrovert. He had a fierce reputation for being a temperamental, authoritarian and a larger-than-life character. His re-editing of *A Digest of Ham* (which he effectively stole out of the clutches of a colleague because he believed he could do a better job), is full of his acerbic wit and general derogatory attitudes to anyone non-British. It was, however, a very equal xenophobia as it covered just about every race under the sun and some of it was done with a very tongue-in-cheek delight at provocation.

He was a man of dual personalities; on the one hand he was short tem-pered with men he thought were working for the enemy, on the other he was considered a generous and kind boss, thought of very fondly by his staff. He was also known for his generosity at the monthly mess parties, where food and drink were available in copious amounts.

Stephens was a career soldier. Born to British parents in Egypt in 1900, he came to Britain aged 12. By the age of 18 he had joined the Royal Military Academy, Woolwich, later transferring to a cadet college in India and finally serving with the Indian army. He served in five campaigns on the North-West Frontier, took part in the Mahbar Rebellion and was even Mentioned in Despatches. Parts of his history are a little hazy, and his First World War service has vague gaps. After the war he was still in India serving on the country's political service, before moving on to become a magis-trate and then an assistant judge-advocate-general. On 9 September 1939, Stephens joined the security service as a captain.

He was a typical MI5 candidate: a veteran of the First World War, part of the old boys' network and a member of the armed services. Yet Stephens' vague history in India suggests he was already something of a secretive person and may have already dabbled in espionage or intelligence gathering.

Versed in a number of languages (Urdu, Arabic, Somali, Amharic, French, German, Italian) he still maintained the aura of a British gentleman and army officer. He had travelled widely, despite his disapproval of most for-eign nationals. Of particular interest to the wartime MI5 were his travels in France, Germany and Italy. He spent a spell in England in 1933 when he became inexplicably attached to the courts at Lincoln's Inn; although he never becoming a lawyer, he collaborated on a book about the laws and evidence of courts martial (a book that could have come back to haunt him in 1948). Adding to his list of odd contrasts, he had spent time as a journalist developing the writing style that would come to the fore in *A Digest of Ham*, while also taking an unofficial role in the Italian–Abyssinian crisis, earning himself the Star of Abyssinia. Then, between 1937 and 1939, he was working for the National Fitness Council of England! It seems Stephens' life was as odd and extroverted as he was.

It is again not clear (what is in this man's life?) what his early days at MI5 were like, but by 1940 he was pushing, along with others, for a dedicated interrogation camp to be set up; this would ultimately become Camp 020.

In contrast there was Lieutenant Colonel Scotland, the middle son of a large and extended Scottish family. He had none of the old boys' network behind him; he left school at 14 and had intentions of travelling abroad with no real purpose except a boyhood fantasy of exploring. He ended up working for a commercial merchants' office and spending a year at the age of 17 in Australia. When he returned to England he found work with the London grocery business of John Sainsbury, but it wasn't long before an itch to travel resurfaced and he was planning to sail to South Africa with ambitions of taking part in the Boer War. Like so much of Scotland's life it was to be a disappointment; he arrived in Africa in time to see the war being wrapped up and ended up working in another grocery store for South African Territories Ltd.

This would prove the turning point in Scotland's life, although even he could not have imagined it at the time. Success as an interrogator involved knowledge of the people you were interviewing and for Scotland this came in South Africa, where he not only learned German but developed a great understanding of the German culture and, in particular, military organisation. His moment came not long after he arrived in the country; part of his role as a grocer was to supply the German soldiers stationed not far away. The arrangement was a little awkward as he was British and a civilian so he was asked to join the German army as a supplies officer. Scotland hardly hesitated in agreeing and became a War Volunteer but with officers' mess status.

In his autobiography, Scotland proudly writes that this was a cunning ploy on his side to enable him to study the Germans more fully:

While I handed out the sweets, biscuits and non-alcoholic drinks, I was perfecting my German and studying the Germans. The Prime Minister of the Cape Colony, Dr L.S. Jameson eventually asked to see me and questioned me about the Germans. Soon I was gathering information on an informal basis for British Intelligence in Cape Town. Something my German comrades failed to realise.[1]

There was never anything humble about Scotland and he always took great pride in explaining his cunning career as a freelance spy. Working, as he did, in an intelligence world populated by public schoolboys of well-connected families and high-flying military careers, it perhaps can be understood that the Scottish working-class lad within the colonel felt the need to inflate his own worth. But to the ears of his readers this eloquent bravado rings a little untrue. In 1904 could the 22-year-old Scotland really have formulated this plan of gathering information in anticipation of a world war? There is no doubt that Germany was unpopular in the British mind at that time. The Boer War (with the kaiser sending a congratulatory telegram to the president of the South African Republic on the defeat of a British raid) had left many with anti-German feelings. Scotland never professed to be one of them, but he had no qualms gathering information on his newly befriended comrades.

'At the time intelligence was my little "hobby", I became known as Schottland to the Germans and was trusted almost everywhere. At some point they did grow suspicious, perhaps I was spotted walking through an ordnance depot taking photographs of secret new German guns, or someone noticed that my trips to Cape Town were not confined to just visiting my employer's head office. But they never found out the truth.'[2]

The First World War changed everything and Scotland spent a year in a South African prison due to trumped-up charges designed by the Germans to get rid of the British from the country. He eventually made it home and decided to join up via British intelligence.

'I was turned down by the War Office because they said there were no vacancies. The Naval department said I was too old. I finally got in via the Inns of Court Infantry Battalion when I unashamedly used a well-known general to recommend me.'[3]

You can feel the tinge of hurt in Scotland's words – he was not eagerly recruited like so many of his comrades, he had to barter his way in, and all this when he felt he had already been serving his country so proficiently and was one of the best intelligence men they would ever find. The chip that invariably loitered on Scotland's shoulder definitely had its origins in the rejections he faced during this time.

Even when he apologises for the War Office's failure to recognise his potential, it is with bitterness:

> You see I was short. Physically I looked half as tough as I truly was. My voice was rather flat and colourless, and I had a face that seemed easily forgotten. Indeed, I was, and still am, an unusually ordinary looking individual. Not that those attributes, if such they can be called, have ever displeased me, for in the world of espionage and security they are a man's finest asset; a defensive camouflage of immeasurable value.[4]

Indeed, from later pictures available of Scotland, you can see exactly why he didn't strike an imposing impression on the War Office interview panels. He looked old for his uniform (like he was trying it on for old times' sake), his hair had turned white and he had an appearance of being inoffensive and harmless. It is hard to view him from his snapshots as a man that has been accused of torturing prisoners in his charge.

Yet behind the round, thick glasses and the wispy smile there was a hardness that had arisen from Scotland's time in the intelligence service. He had seen comrades turn on each other, argued with seemingly decent British men who praised Hitler and had met the Führer himself. Before the First World War was over he had grown cold towards his former German friends and comrades.

'After the First World War I regularly had contact with Germans in both South Africa and South America, I also travelled to the country itself. I saw firsthand the German war machine coming together, the secret armies, the forming of SS and Gestapo. I even met Hitler.'[5]

That was one aspect of his life that Scotland could feel no pride for. Perhaps if he had managed to get some vital information from Hitler he might have praised the encounter for his own ingenuity, but instead he found himself at the mercy of the most evil man of the modern age. It was a surprise meeting at an old German friend's house; Scotland never knew why the Führer wanted to meet him, but it was obviously an orchestrated event. Hitler had him sit where the full glare of the sun hit his face while they drank coffee from silver cups. The Führer quizzed him on his time in the German army in South Africa and his opinions on the current situation in the country, in particular, on Hitler's views that South West Africa should come back under direct German control. When the interview was over Hitler rose and strode to the doorway, pausing for a moment to say: 'You are an ingenious man Schottland. Now I can understand the reports we have on file about you.'

Whether this is true or a bluff on Scotland's part to comfort himself about the whole ordeal is difficult to say. Scotland always gave the impression of a man eager to emphasize the significance of his role in the war. In fact, speaking to him you could almost form the impression that he single-handedly devised and organised the British intelligence system; he certainly liked to paint himself as a pivotal figure, which some of his superiors would have argued over.

The result of dipping into Scotland's background is a profound under-standing of how an adventurous youth went from spying as a game to developing a deep and bitter dislike for the German military and those who served Nazism. You can read his thoughts as he writes with distaste about the 'ugly arrangements for murder, of which there were plenty', referring to the concentration camps and the removal of Nazi dissenters. No doubt as he penned that he would have reflected on his own time in that African prison, the cold, calm, calculating men who put him there, and the unsmil-ing Hitler who invited him to coffee so he might be interrogated.

From these two portraits of the most influential men in the interrogation system it can be seen why they rose to such success and, equally, why one then fell and the other teetered on the brink. Scotland turned his hatred to torture; Stephens recognised the futility of giving in to this emotion. They are both names that will live on in the history of Second World War intel-ligence, for better or worse.

The Brainwashing Professor

There is one name that has mostly escaped the controversy and blacklist-ing that Scotland and Stephens still often face in the press. Yet this man could be accused of equal sadism, as he led the way for brainwashing techniques and created another black mark on the interrogators' record. He only surfaced in 1960, at a time when many perhaps felt the controversies of that aspect of the war had died down. His name was Professor Alexander Kennedy, and when he stood up to give a lecture in London on the effects of brainwashing POWs during interrogation, the highly respected Professor of Psychological Medicine at Edinburgh instantly caused a huge amount of controversy with his allegations of drugs, hypnosis and sensory deprivation being used on prisoners to get them to talk.

In 1960, Labour MP Mr John Cronin tabled a question for the prime minister to be answered in the House of Commons. It asked: 'If employees of any government department, including the secret service, have during the last twenty years employed the psychological technique of inducing in prisoners disintegration of personality, followed by emotional attachment to an interrogator, that is, the process commonly known as brainwashing, for the purpose of obtaining confessions from prisoners or influencing their future conduct?'[6]

It was a dark moment; Cronin was adamant that the British public needed to know if such abhorrent practices had been going on under their noses. Cronin referred to recent fears on the invasion of privacy by phone-tapping and stated his question was only to ensure the British public had the confidence to know that further incursions on their personal liberties were not being made.

Kennedy claimed his information was all hypotheses and his lecture was actually about applying wartime interrogation techniques to the treatment of psychiatric illnesses. The British press, however, started to shout that Kennedy must have had insider knowledge of such techniques and that the British secret service must have been using them on enemy agents. Again Kennedy denied the charges; he had, he admitted, worked for British intelligence during the war, but nothing representing a brainwashing technique was ever used.

The problem had now gone past the stage when denials by Kennedy would be sufficient. On 9 March 1960 there was a House of Commons debate on the subject where the Secretary of State for War came under a harrowing range of questions, all firmly fixed on the belief that brainwashing had been (and possibly still was) used by the army. The Secretary made ardent denials, even reading out a letter from Professor Kennedy where the psychologist stated he had deduced his material for the lecture from a number of books and magazines and had never once mentioned that Britain had used the method. The rampaging critics were not happy; the Secretary was harangued into a corner until he finally admitted that certain divisions of the army were taught brainwashing techniques, not to use them, but to be prepared if they were used against them.

The whole matter had exploded into a national argument with no one knowing the truth. To quell the storm, Prime Minister Harold Macmillan finally stated during prime minister's questions that at no time had such methods been used by an organisation answerable to Her Majesty's government. That firm statement, followed by the death of Professor Kennedy three months after he gave his talk, seemed to put an end to the growing furore, at least in the public eye.

In private, Kennedy's words had stirred others to come forward. MP Francis Noel-Baker, who had served with British intelligence during the war, wrote to the prime minister: 'It is within my own personal knowledge, and that of people with whom I served during the war, that a technique of brainwashing was certainly used by Major Kennedy, as he then was, and other interrogators at the [CSDIC], outside Cairo, during the last war.'[7]

Other evidence started to trickle out over the years, including a document penned by Sir Dick White (head of MI6), who had witnessed such methods being used and stated that Kennedy had been the psychological advisor at such interrogations. One was of an Egyptian man, Ellie Haggar, suspected of being a German spy. He was plied with drugs, but the result was disappointing as they just made him even more unapproachable for questioning and he eventually contracted pneumonia. White had put forth his opinion that such techniques were useless. But even among men who had worked at CSDIC Cairo the debate was still far from over; some simply could not believe that men they had worked so closely with had dabbled with such methods. It is probable that only a handful of interrogators under the supervision of Kennedy (and it seems conclusive that he was involved in brainwashing) ever took part in the experiments, and the poor results would have put paid to the scheme quickly. Yet it is sad to think that those men even chose to take that route. Unfortunately, a few arrogant, misguided souls tend to tarnish a whole service and those who served diligently and humanely get forgotten in the swell of controversy.

Spy Masters and Secretaries

At some point most of the Nazi elite (at least, not those who had murdered themselves rather than face defeat) had stood before an interrogator, often British ones. One such infamous figure was Ernst Kaltenbrunner, the head of the German intelligence branch, RSHA, and the highest-ranking SS officer to be tried at Nuremberg. An Austrian by birth, the lean-faced Kaltenbrunner, with his duelling scars, had risen in the Nazi Party ranks, even replacing the high-ranking Nazi official Reinhard Heydrich after his assassination. From 1944 he had direct access to the Führer and worked on mock trials to eliminate those deemed to have plotted the attempt on Hitler's life earlier in the year. It was rumoured that his volatile nature and imposing presence even had Himmler in fear and awe of him.

By 1945, with defeat looming, Himmler named Kaltenbrunner commander-in-chief of the remaining German forces in southern Europe. His new role didn't deter him from fleeing his headquarters in Berlin in April of that year, however, keeping just ahead of the Americans until May when he was accosted and caught.

Kaltenbrunner was 'loaned' to the British while awaiting trial at Nuremberg so they might find out more about the RSHA. No man had ever tested Stephens' patience and self-control as Kaltenbrunner did when he arrived at Camp 020. A swaggering, arrogant man, Stephens later wrote that it was only necessary to be in his presence and hear him speak for a person to realise the evil in this one man. He labelled him a brute and mused that it was obvious to see his appeal to Hitler; 'he had brain, brawn, ruthlessness and a certain suavity to offset the overall impression of frightfulness'.[8]

Kaltenbrunner was a tough nut to crack. He had no intention of talking to the British about anything; he knew the charges hanging over his head and that he was only to be in the interrogators' hands for a short period before he was transferred to Nuremberg. He took that confidence and presented an unshakeable façade of silence; fortunately he had his weaknesses. His main one was blackmail, something he had used gladly against others in his service. Stephens had learned that the married Kaltenbrunner had twins by a mistress and he threatened to expose the whole sordid affair and ruin the lives of everyone involved. It was a low blow, and although it caused Kaltenbrunner to open up for a time, he soon shut down again.

Exasperated, Stephens had to fall back on other sources, namely fellow inmates of Camp 020 who had a reason to dislike the arrogant Nazi. Some were former employees of the mighty Kaltenbrunner, who now felt betrayed and provided everything they could about the man to the British. There were also camp agents who worked to undermine the RSHA chief and when Walther Schellenberg, former assistant to Himmler, arrived at Ham he was almost too keen to betray his former chief. Unfortunately, it was simply not enough; Kaltenbrunner knew the interrogators were on short time and he held out, eventually being removed to Nuremberg without providing the goldmine of information the British had hoped for.

It might have been some consolation for Stephens and his team, had they known how difficult Kaltenbrunner also proved for the American interrogators who took over his case at Nuremberg. Kaltenbrunner outright refused to accept any responsibility for the Gestapo (Department IV of his RSHA) or their programme of genocide. He made flamboyant and determined arguments that it simply wasn't his fault and even when faced with documents, charts and affidavits that proved beyond a shadow of a doubt that he had been responsible for the deaths of millions, he simply refused to accept it.

One of Kaltenbrunner's accusers, Walther Schellenberg, also took a metaphorical pummelling at Camp 020. He was only too eager to rat out the RSHA chief who he in part owed his job to. He had hoped to play the part of an Allied insider; giving the appearance of a man who had served Hitler only to bring about his destruction. In that sense he made a calculated error by speaking out against Kaltenbrunner, who, for once, had no hesitation in talking about the blue-eyed former head of the Amt VI.

Schellenberg had been playing a dangerous game of skin-saving; on the one hand towing the Nazi Party line and on the other trying to ensure his security and future when the Allies won the war. He had tried to bring about world peace (or so he claimed) via an amateur Swedish diplomat named Count Bernadotte. When that had inevitably failed he went to the Americans to rat out his former bosses Kaltenbrunner and Himmler, and thus he ended up at Camp 020 being used, unsuccessfully, as a tool against the former RSHA head.

Stephens had nothing but contempt for the 'priggish little dandy' who washed up at his door, and Schellenberg was stunned by the grim reception he faced; he had expected at least a comradely welcome as he was a 'friend' to the Allies, after all. He was even more shocked when he discovered that his little charade was not fooling anyone and that the British knew all about the evil deeds he had done in the name of the Amt VI. He had ruthlessly and efficiently carried out his work for the Nazis, and his attempts to mask his treason failed to fool anyone. Stephens was in fact a touch disappointed he 'was not as good an enemy as Kaltenbrunner'.

Another spymaster who fell into the CSDIC's lap was Oberstleutnant Nikolaus Ritter. He had become a notorious name during the early years of the war, but had started his espionage career in 1937 when he left his adopted homeland of America and took a position working for the German military. He had been recruited by the German military attaché in Washington after the collapse of his textile business, and no one was more surprised than Ritter when he was assigned to the Abwehr and given the role of Chief of Air Intelligence. Suddenly, he was working against the country he had lived and worked in for so long, but that didn't stop him.

Ritter became one of the benefactors of the Double-Cross System the British devised, particularly through the agent Snow who in fact was hardly loyal to anyone. The British kept track of Ritter's progress; his career in the Sonderkommando planting spies in the desert and his later command of the anti-aircraft defences of Hannover. Stephens enjoyed recounting how Bomber Harris had completely fooled Ritter with a feint, when a large group of Bomber Command flew over Hannover apparently heading for another target. The nervous Ritter, who was always better with his spies than big guns, stood down his men, only to find that the planes were returning and the devastation they wreaked was immeasurable.

It was Ritter's connection with the double agent Snow that caused British intelligence both great pleasure and anxiety. Snow's German cover name was 'Johnny', while Ritter always met him in the guise of 'Dr Rantzau'. Snow was perhaps the most dangerous double agent because he was loyal neither to his German masters nor the British. He happily betrayed whoever took his fancy, while also providing truth and evidence for whichever master he liked at the moment. He was betraying everyone and both sides still endowed him with absurd faith and trust. Even after the war, when Ritter was captured by MI5, he was still under the impression that 'Johnny' was a loyal German spy.

During Ritter's stay in the hands of the CSDIC he proved relatively co-operative and gave a lengthy account of his experiences with the Abwehr, even if some of his memories were tainted by the lapse of time. He admitted that he was not the greatest of intelligence officers, but with a certain amount of bootlicking put that down to British secret service superiority rather than his own incompetence. Once trapped and cornered, he became something of a tame mouse and eventually usurped a German general who commanded a squad of prisoners employed in cleaning the officers' mess. Stephens caustically wrote, 'in this way he can dream of the Guest Nights of the past and distribute the cigarette ends of today.'

Alongside Ritter was another Abwehr man, Ahlrichs, a kapitänleutnant, who had been a leading figure for five years in the marine section of the spy organisation. He had been responsible for despatching agents by sea via U-boats or small craft. Then there was Lahousen, an Abwehr agent who had fallen with Admiral Canaris. Angered by defeat, he surrendered papers to the Americans who first held him, and then he went on to testify against the criminals at Nuremberg. He ended up at CSDIC in Germany a bitter and repentant man; hated by the German nation for betraying the army he once so loyally served, shunned by his fellow inmates and held in contempt by the British. He was a typical example of the anguished turncoat now facing the fact he was despised on all sides.

Gestapo Men and Genocidal Maniacs

It was inevitable that with the conclusion of the war the darkest elements of Nazi Germany would finally be routed and driven into the clutches of MI5. The chapters of the interrogation files, so long concerned with espionage and military secrets, now turned into something more reminiscent of a horror novel.

Horst Kopkow was just such a dark element. Responsible for the deaths of hundreds of Allied agents, he was an SS major working for the German National Security Police, mainly dealing with counter-sabotage and counter-espionage. Kopkow organised the rounding up of enemy agents who had been parachuted into the country, including members of MI6. Each successful capture by his men was reported directly to his headquarters in

Berlin and he had the final say on their sentence – invariably death. He even investigated the 20 July assassination plot on Hitler. By the end of the war he was a heavily decorated officer, with a lot of Allied blood on his hands.

British military police captured him in a Baltic village in May of 1945 and passed him over to intelligence. He should have been prosecuted as he was implicated in at least 300 Allied agents' deaths, but he proved such a valuable source on methods to counter Soviet espionage that he was protected from being sent to trial by the secret service. For four years he shared his insider knowledge with the interrogators and they so valued his help that they officially declared his death to the War Crimes group in 1948 so that he would no longer be hunted on that front. Instead, in 1949 or 1950, it seems he was released into West Germany where he worked in a textile factory – a very inglorious end for such a high-flying National Socialist. He is thought to have died of pneumonia in 1996.

A man who was not about to be granted such liberties was Oswald Pohl, a high-ranking Nazi and SS man responsible for the murder of millions of Jews in concentration camps. In Bad Nenndorf he proved unrepentant. Genocide had been his mission, murder his government's creed, and he was happy to carry it out as he agreed with it wholeheartedly. It seems he never had any regrets about the many lives he had destroyed, though he took his time to agree to a final figure on the men, women and children he had massacred – he compromised to between 3,000,000 and 20,000,000 human beings.

Originally serving in the German navy during the First World War, he eventually transferred to the SS and became a generalleutnant. He looks a quiet, humble person in his Nuremberg photo, though the crooked smile on his face, considering the situation he was in, belies an ingrained arrogance. Pohl was eventually responsible for the administration of the concentration camps and the mounting deaths he endorsed led him to the hangman's noose. Stephens was glad to see the back of this man, who he deemed a fanatic and, still so close to the war's end, paused to reflect that men like Pohl had come frighteningly close to achieving their aims of world domination.

A case of reputation over reality was that of Simmross Fiebig. At a distance he seemed a sinister figure, dancing in the shadows of the German war effort. After the war, in Stephens' words, he 'was good enough to accept an unavoidable invitation to CSDIC in Germany'; he rather disappointed the interrogators. He had earned several dishonourable Mentions in Despatches, but when presented to the team at Bad Nenndorf he gave the impression of a gutter-trawling fraud. He even made pretence of having been forced into the secret service by his parents! According to Fiebig, his mother had been particularly fond of the idea and, against his better judgement, he found himself serving the German Embassy as a Wehrmacht interpreter in France. He told his interrogators: 'I don't mind to put me in your hands naked, because you have proved to be right and I felt it is my duty after my mistake.'

What is the story of British interrogation during the war? It was a learning curve, a practice that had to be developed in the space of a few short years, and successfully developed at that. It gave us the foundations for our future intelligence networks and it taught us some valuable lessons. Unfortunately, some of them refuse to be learned.

It was not a perfect system, but remove the errant London Cage and Bad Nenndorf and look at the thousands of prisoners, civilians and spies who faced a British interrogator, and it is obvious that MI5, CSDIC and the British military were developing an efficient and ethical system – one that did not rely on torture or brutality to achieve its ends. The fact that some men faltered and that the evidence they gained was far poorer than that achieved by their non-violent colleagues, only goes to illustrate why torture is the pathetic resort of an ignorant man. A resort that leads to far more failures. A resort that, if it does produce results, has those results disbelieved by those who hear how they were extracted. In short, it is pointless.

Britain had one of the finest interrogation systems of the Second World War; they broke men, they got results and, it is not over exaggerating to say, that triumphant system enabled them to win the war. They were so impressive even the Germans began to copy them, at least in those divisions not hooked on violence and abuse.

Perhaps the best, final comment on British interrogation and intelligence during the war comes from an America author, Ladislas Farago, on his research of the Abwehr: 'When I started my researches, I thought the Germans had probably won the espionage war. When I finished them, I knew it was the British.'

That triumph was in large part due to the humble work of interrogators, microphone operators, typists and interpreters, who worked in secret and whose story still remains so mysterious today. They were the people who won the war.

Notes
1 Lieutenant Colonel A.P. Scotland OBE, *The London Cage*.
2 Ibid.
3 Ibid.
4 Ibid.
5 Ibid.
6 'MP to ask about Brainwashing', in *The Times*, Monday, 14 March 1960.
7 'Britain's WWII Brainwashing', BBC News *http://news.bbc.co.uk/1/hi/uk/8361655.stm*.
8 Lieutenant Colonel Stephens (ed.), *A Digest of Ham*.

BIBLIOGRAPHY

Baillie-Stewart, Norman, *The Officer in the Tower*, Leslie Frewin Publishers, 1967

Basoglu, Metin (ed.), *Torture and its Consequences: Current Treatment Approaches*, Cambridge University Press, 1992

Bernstein, Jeremy, *Hitler's Uranium Club: The Secret Recordings at Farm Hall*, Springer, 2001

Burt, Kendal & Leasor, James, *The One that Got Away*, Collins, 1956

Crankshaw, Edward, *Gestapo, Instrument of Tyranny*, Wren Park Publishing, 2002

Farago, Ladislas, *The Game of the Foxes: British and German Intelligence Operations and Personalities which Changed the Course of the Second World War*, Hodder & Stoughton, 1971

Haufler, Hervie, *The Spies Who Never Were*, EReads, 2011

Knöchlein, Fritz, *The London Cage: The Experiences of Fritz Knöchlein*, Steven Books, 2008

Luenberger, David G., *Information Science*, Princeton University Press, 2008

Marshall, Bruce, *The White Rabbit*, Evans Brothers, 1952

Nebeker, Frederik, *Dawn of the Electronic Age: Electrical Technologies in the Shaping of the Modern World, 1914 to 1945*, Wiley-Blackwell, 2009

Overy, Richard, *Interrogations: the Nazi Elite in Allied Hands 1945*, The Penguin Press, 2001

Palevsky, Mary, *Atomic Fragments: A Daughter's Questions*, University of California Press, 2000

Scotland, Lieutenant Colonel A.P., *The London Cage*, Evans Brothers, 1957

Stephens, Lieutenant Colonel (ed.), *A Digest of Ham: Volume One, A Digest of Ham on the Interrogation of Spies 1940–47*

Thiessen, Mark A., *Courting Disaster: How the CIA kept America Safe and how Barack Obama is inviting the next Attack*, Regnery Publishing Inc., 2010

Thomson, Sir Basil, *The Scene Changes*, Country Life Press, USA, 1937

West, Nigel (ed.), *The Guy Liddell Diaries: 1942–1945, Vol 2*, Routledge, 2005

Documents and Other Sources

'Alleged Malingerer at Bad Nenndorf', in *The Times*, Tuesday, 13 April 1948

'Attack by German Tanks in Tunisia', in *The Times*, Monday, 1 February 1943

'German Tanks Beaten Off', in *The Times*, Saturday, 6 February 1943

'German Tanks Mass, Preparations for a New Drive', in *The Times*, Tuesday, 28 July 1942

'MP to ask about Brainwashing', in *The Times*, Monday, 14 March 1960

'Tanks and Guns, Rival Armaments in Libya, The German Lead', in *The Times*, Saturday, 27 June 1942

'Tanks and Guns, German and British Design, Power of Manoeuvre', in *The Times*, Monday, 29 June 1942

Bernin, Michel, 'Konigstein Prison', in *Life*, 21 September 1942

'The Battle of the Tanks', in *Life*, 26 March 1945

'Airborne Troops Retreat from Arnhem', *On This Day; 26 September 1944*, BBC News *http://news.bbc.co.uk/onthisday/hi/dates/stories/september/26/newsid_3523000/3523972.stm*

'Britain's WWII Brainwashing', BBC News *http://news.bbc.co.uk/1/hi/uk/8361655.stm*

Sheffield, Dr Gary, 'The Battle of the Atlantic: The U-boat Peril', BBC History *www.bbc.co.uk/history/worldwars/wwtwo/battle_atlantic_01.shtml*

'Germany finally honours the "traitor" who gave Nazi secrets to America', in *The Independent*, Saturday, 25 September 2004

Interrogation files held at The National Archives, WO208/4117-4197

MI5 official history *www.mi5.gov.uk/output/history.html*

INDEX

Other titles published by The History Press

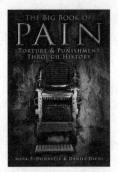

The Big Book of Pain: Torture & Punishment through History

MARK P. DONNELLY & DANIEL DIEHL

9780752459479

For millennia, mankind has devised ingenious and diabolical means of inflicting pain on fellow human beings. Despite how the practice of torture appears to us today, for at least 3,000 years it formed part of most legal codes. *The Big Book of Pain* is an exploration of the systematic use throughout the ages of punishment, torture and coercion. From the ancient Roman Coliseum and the medieval dungeon to the witch-trial and the prison.

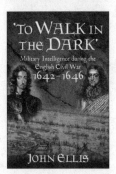

To Walk in the Dark: Military Intelligence in the English Civil War, 1642–1646

JOHN ELLIS

9780752460239

During the bloody years of the first English Civil War, as the battles of Edgehill, Newbury and Naseby raged, another war was being fought. Its combatants fought with cunning and deceit, a hidden conflict that nevertheless would steer the course of history. The story of the spies and intelligence-gatherers of the Roundheads and Royalists is one that sheds new light on the birth of the Commonwealth.

Heroines of SOE: F Section: Britain's Secret Women in France

SQUADRON LEADER BERYL E. ESCOTT

9780752463131

The history of SOE's war in the shadows has been told many times and much is known about the men who fought underground. However, less is known about the women who also risked their lives for Britain and the liberation of France. Without doubt their contributions to Britain's secret missions of intelligence-gathering and sabotage helped the resistance to drive out their occupiers and free France. Here, for the first time, is their story.

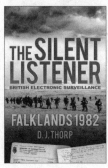

The Silent Listener – Falklands 1982: British Electronic Surveillance

MAJOR D.J. THORP

9780752460291

On 2 April 1982 Argentina launched Operation Rosario, the invasion of the Falklands. The British, caught off guard, responded with Operation Corporate. Deployed alongside the rest of the British army was a small specialist intelligence unit, whose very existence was unknown to many commanders and whose activities were cloaked in the Official Secrets Act. Trained during the years of the Cold War, the OC of the unit, D.J. Thorp, recounts their story.

Visit our website and discover thousands of other History Press books.

www.thehistorypress.co.uk